# THE MARMON GROUP
## THE FIRST FIFTY YEARS

# THE MARMON GROUP
## THE FIRST FIFTY YEARS

# JEFFREY L. RODENGEN

Edited by Jon VanZile
Design and layout by Dennis Shockley and Wendy Iverson

Write Stuff Enterprises, Inc.
1001 South Andrews Avenue
Second Floor
Fort Lauderdale, FL 33316
**1-800-900-Book** (1-800-900-2665)
954-462-6657
www.writestuffbooks.com

Copyright © 2002 by Write Stuff Enterprises, Inc. All rights reserved. No part of this book may be reproduced or transmitted in any form by any means, electronic or mechanical, including photocopying and recording, or by any information storage or retrieval system, without permission in writing from the publisher.

**Publisher's Cataloging in Publication**

Rodengen, Jeffrey L.
    The Marmon Group: the first fifty years/
Jeffrey L. Rodengen; edited by Jon VanZile;
design and layout by Dennis Shockley and
Wendy Iverson. – 1st ed.
    p. cm.
    Includes bibliographical references and index.
    LCCN 00136031
    ISBN 0-945903-77-4

    1. Marmon Group – History. 2. Manufacturing industries – United States – History. I. VanZile, Jon. II. Title.

HD9729.M37R632 2002        338.7'67'0977311
                                            QBI02-200605

Library of Congress
Catalog Card Number 00136031

ISBN 0-945903-77-4

Completely produced in the
United States of America
10 9 8 7 6 5 4 3 2 1

Frontispiece: Bob Pritzker, who with his brother Jay created The Marmon Group. Today the organization has more than 100 member companies and more than $6 billion in worldwide revenue.

# Also by Jeffrey L. Rodengen

*The Legend of Chris-Craft*

*IRON FIST: The Lives of Carl Kiekhaefer*

*Evinrude-Johnson and The Legend of OMC*

*Serving the Silent Service: The Legend of Electric Boat*

*The Legend of Dr Pepper/Seven-Up*

*The Legend of Honeywell*

*The Legend of Briggs & Stratton*

*The Legend of Ingersoll-Rand*

*The Legend of Stanley: 150 Years of The Stanley Works*

*The MicroAge Way*

*The Legend of Halliburton*

*The Legend of York International*

*The Legend of Nucor Corporation*

*The Legend of Goodyear: The First 100 Years*

*The Legend of AMP*

*The Legend of Cessna*

*The Legend of VF Corporation*

*The Spirit of AMD*

*The Legend of Rowan*

*New Horizons: The Story of Ashland Inc.*

*The History of American Standard*

*The Legend of Mercury Marine*

*The Legend of Federal-Mogul*

*Against the Odds: Inter-Tel—The First 30 Years*

*The Legend of Pfizer*

*State of the Heart: The Practical Guide to Your Heart and Heart Surgery*
with Larry W. Stephenson, M.D.

*The Legend of Worthington Industries*

*The Legend of Trinity Industries, Inc.*

*The Legend of IBP, Inc.*

*The Legend of Cornelius Vanderbilt Whitney*

*The Legend of Amdahl*

*The Legend of Litton Industries*

*The Legend of Gulfstream*

*The Legend of Bertram*
with David A. Patten

*The Legend of Ritchie Bros. Auctioneers*

*The Legend of ALLTEL*
with David A. Patten

*The Yes, you can of Invacare Corporation*
with Anthony L. Wall

*The Ship in the Balloon: The Story of Boston Scientific and the Development of Less-Invasive Medicine*

*The Legend of Day & Zimmermann*

*The Legend of Noble Drilling*

*50 Years of Innovation: Kulicke & Soffa*

*Biomet—From Warsaw to the World*
with Richard F. Hubbard

*NRA: An American Legend*

*The Heritage and Values of RPM, Inc.*

# TABLE OF CONTENTS

Introduction . . . . . . . . . . . . . . . . . . . . . . . . . . . . . . . . . . . . . . . . vi

Acknowledgments . . . . . . . . . . . . . . . . . . . . . . . . . . . . . . . . . . . ix

## Section I

| | | |
|---|---|---|
| Chapter I | Brothers in Business | 12 |
| Chapter II | The Marmon Group Is Born | 28 |
| Chapter III | Consolidating Gains | 42 |
| Chapter IV | The End of the Beginning | 50 |

## Section II

| | | |
|---|---|---|
| Chapter V | The Marmon Framework | 68 |
| Chapter VI | Services | 74 |
| Chapter VII | Industry | 82 |
| Chapter VIII | Medical & Water Products | 96 |
| Chapter IX | Transportation | 108 |
| Chapter X | Metals | 124 |

Notes to Sources . . . . . . . . . . . . . . . . . . . . . . . . . . . . . . . . . . . 140

Index . . . . . . . . . . . . . . . . . . . . . . . . . . . . . . . . . . . . . . . . . . . 152

# INTRODUCTION

IN 1953, BROTHERS BOB AND JAY Pritzker bought the Colson Corporation, a troubled manufacturing company in Elyria, Ohio. It was their first acquisition and represented a tremendous challenge. Colson operated from a sprawling jungle of antiquated buildings, some dating back almost a century, and made products that ranged from bicycles to wheelchairs to industrial casters to rockets for the U.S. Navy.

It was an unlikely turnaround candidate—but the Pritzkers were an unusual combination. Sons of a distinguished Chicago attorney, A. N. Pritzker, the brothers had complementary strengths uniquely suited to buying and turning around companies like Colson.

Jay Pritzker was a financial wizard, a master of tax law and the art of the deal. In the 1950s, while building The Marmon Group with Bob, he perfected a way to finance acquisitions by using a loophole in the tax code; in fact, the "Pritzker method" became its nickname. Jay Pritzker was also universally respected as a savvy negotiator.

Bob Pritzker was the first engineer in a family of lawyers. He had a knack and a passion for plant management and by the age of twenty-four, before they bought Colson, had already become general manager of a manufacturing company.

When the Pritzker brothers bought Colson, they laid the groundwork for a partnership and an organization that would grow by leaps and bounds over the years. But first there was the issue of what to do with their new company. Shortly after they acquired it, Bob moved to Ohio to take over the byzantine network of buildings and turn it into a profitable, modern operation. Before long, through a complicated series of acquisitions, the Pritzker brothers financed Colson's move from Ohio to a brand new plant in Arkansas.

Thus began the story of The Marmon Group. In the annals of corporate America, The Marmon Group is unique. It is a loose federation of companies, a nonlegal entity that shares only the distinction of being controlled by the Pritzker family. The Marmon Group comprises mostly manufacturing companies that operate across a broad spectrum of American industry. The list of Marmon member companies includes stalwarts such as Trans Union, Union Tank Car, Marmon/Keystone, Cerro Copper Products, Cerro Metal Products, Cerro Wire & Cable, L. A. Darling, EcoWater Systems, and Webb Wheel, among many others.

The member companies of The Marmon Group are a manufacturing force to be reckoned with. The more than one hundred companies have revenue in excess of $6 billion and produce a mind-boggling array of products. The Marmon Group operates more than 200 factories and employs about 35,000 in forty-five countries. The largest company, Trans Union, is among the most recognizable consumer credit companies in the world.

The Marmon Group is not notable for its size alone, however. As Jay and Bob Pritzker gradually added to the organization, Bob laid down ground rules that remain in place today. Marmon Group member companies are managed independently, at the local level, and a dual reporting structure feeds financial results to The Marmon Group's Chicago office, where each member company is tracked closely by a small cadre of executives and managers. Beyond that, most operating and capital decisions are entrusted to the individual company presidents. Even acquisitions are often handled at the local level.

If the need arises, however, the Chicago staff comprises a group of corporate experts who are available to member companies for advice and guidance on issues like tax law, human resources, environmental regulations, and the myriad other concerns that confront businesses.

These services are available to member companies on a consulting basis and represent a powerful inducement to join The Marmon Group. A member of The Marmon Group has access to tremendous resources and expertise over a wide spectrum. These resources have been put to good use: although the enterprise was built through acquisition, much of its growth over the years has been internal.

This basic approach has proved remarkably resilient. Although The Marmon Group has evolved in recent years, it has remained surprisingly stable. Although new acquisitions are common, few companies are sold.

Similarly, turnover among member company presidents is minimal, and the staff in the corporate office has remained stable over the decades. And while The Marmon Group has made some efforts in recent years to gain advantage from its sheer size, the basic decentralized operating structure remains intact. Marmon companies are not forced into buying consortiums, and they do not leverage themselves off one another unless it makes sense from a business point of view.

Despite the regularity of its operation, The Marmon Group is not without drama. Its creation, which took place mostly between the 1953 acquisition of Colson and 1981, when the Pritzkers arranged the purchase of Trans Union, is a story of acquisitive brilliance and corporate turnaround.

Over the years, the brothers polished their approach to buying companies and growing their businesses. The ideal candidate for The Marmon Group was a manufacturing company, preferably one that was ailing and needed to be revitalized. In the beginning, no attention was given to what business the company operated in and whether it would fit well with existing member companies. What mattered more was that the company represented a solid opportunity.

Once a target had been identified, Jay typically would make the deal, and then Bob would run the place. Bob's bailiwick was management, encompassing everything from accounting to product development to the shop floor to distribution. Especially in the beginning, Bob would take over a business himself, as he had Colson. As the organization grew, he sent trusted lieutenants to help revamp acquired businesses as needed.

The Marmon Group has repeated this pattern hundreds of times, and many acquisitions were attended by high drama. At various times, the Pritzker brothers dealt with rebellious boards of directors and intransigent owners, and at one point they even invested in a wildly profitable warehouse of cocoa beans. Through Marmon Group member companies, the Pritzker brothers have owned farms, run nationalized plants, and contracted with the U.S. armed forces, and one Marmon Group member company has manufactured the torch that carries the Olympic flame.

Through their work with The Marmon Group, the Pritzker brothers have also made lasting contributions to the science of corporate acquisitions, especially through the Trans Union purchase. This highly charged transaction resulted in a shareholder lawsuit against the Trans Union board over the potential value of the acquisition (the Pritzker brothers were not part of the suit). The resulting judgment was a groundbreaking precedent that shook the foundations of corporate America. At the time, it was covered widely in the business and law media as one of the most significant business-related judgments ever handed down.

Today, The Marmon Group is the Pritzker family's largest enterprise, no small feat in a family that owns the Hyatt Hotels brand and a large interest in Royal Caribbean Cruise Line. Yet its Chicago office remains remarkably small, moving in the same patterns and sticking to the same principles that Bob and Jay Pritzker established decades ago. Salespeople who call on The Marmon Group in downtown Chicago and expect to find the giant headquarters of a corporation are surprised to be ushered into a relatively small office suite.

The Marmon Group has kept thriving and growing because of the integrity and trust built into its most basic structure. Its member companies continue to produce goods that are shipped around the world, and The Marmon Group continues to rank among the largest privately owned enterprises anywhere.

# ACKNOWLEDGMENTS

A GREAT NUMBER OF PEOPLE assisted in the research, preparation, and publication of *The Marmon Group: The First Fifty Years*.

The principal research and narrative time line were the work of Anthony DeBartolo, while the images were collected by Mike Williams. Thanks are also due to Jack Steinberg, whose book, *The Making of The Marmon Group*, provided invaluable insight.

This project would not have been possible without the enthusiastic support of Bob Pritzker, who was generous with his time and his memories of the formative days of The Marmon Group.

David Dees, director of communications, was similarly crucial. His keen eye for detail and his inexhaustible supply of knowledge were both an asset and an encouragement.

Other executives from The Marmon Group, both past and present, also contributed their time, and thanks are extended to all those who helped. They include Ray Avendt, president of Avendt Group, Inc.; Carol D'Ascenzo, a longtime employee of The Marmon Group and secretary of Bob Webb; John Dolan, retired director of industrial relations; Bob Gluth, executive vice president; George Jones, retired executive vice president; Paul Rothgery, retired plant manager of Colson; Gerald Shannon, retired senior vice president; Fred Sitz, former vice president of finance for Colson; and Bob Webb, senior vice president and general counsel.

As always, special thanks are extended to the dedicated staff at Write Stuff Enterprises, Inc.: Richard F. Hubbard, executive author; Jon VanZile, executive editor; Melody Maysonet, senior editor; Heather Deeley, assistant editor; Bonnie Freeman, copyeditor; Mary Aaron, transcriptionist; Barbara Koch, indexer; Sandy Cruz, senior art director; Rachelle Donley, Wendy Iverson, and Dennis Shockley, art directors; Bruce Borich, production manager; Marianne Roberts, vice president of administration; Sherry Hasso, bookkeeper; Linda Edell, executive assistant to the author; Lars Jessen, director of worldwide marketing; Joel Colby, sales and promotions manager; Rory Schmer, distribution supervisor; and Jennifer Walter, administrative assistant.

**1955:** Colson is sold to Great American Industries as the Pritzkers seek control over a new company. This deal eventually finances Colson's move to Jonesboro, Arkansas.

**November 18, 1964:** The Marmon Group is christened as a group of independent companies. That same year, Amarillo Gear Works is acquired.

**1953:** Bob and Jay Pritzker buy the Colson Corporation, an ailing manufacturer in Elyria, Ohio.

**January 1959:** The Pritzkers complete the purchase of the James Mfg. Co. That year, George Jones joins Colson.

1976: Acquisition of Cerro Corporation is completed. The deal more than doubles the size of The Marmon Group.

1981: Acquisition of Trans Union Corporation, a multifaceted public corporation with roots back to John D. Rockefeller's Standard Oil Trust, is completed. The price of the acquisition is $688 million.

1970: Keystone Pipe & Supply Company joins The Marmon Group.

1977: The Marmon Group breaks the billion-dollar sales barrier. Member companies have combined estimated revenues of $1.3 billion.

The Pritzker brothers—Bob, left, and Jay—founders of The Marmon Group.

CHAPTER ONE
# BROTHERS IN BUSINESS
## 1953–1958

*The only reason owners of Colson and other troubled companies sold to us at bargain prices in the early days was because they had no place else to go.*

—Jay Pritzker, 1992

THE BEGINNINGS OF THE Marmon Group can be summed up easily: attorney Jay Arthur Pritzker bought, and engineer Robert Alan Pritzker fixed.

The Marmon Group, an international association of more than one hundred manufacturing and service companies, is held in trust by Chicago's Pritzker family, best known for its other major business: the global Hyatt hotel chain. Like many of the other Pritzker enterprises, The Marmon Group was built from the ground up through internal reinvestment, with virtually no financial investment by the Pritzker family.[1]

Instead, the brothers built the company by shrewdly investing in, and then greatly improving, poorly performing businesses. These were then used as vehicles to purchase yet more businesses, and the process evolved into a role model for building a conglomerate. The first acquisition was the Colson Corporation, bought in 1953, when it was an ailing Ohio metal products firm. Since then, Marmon's growth has been tremendous: in 2000, sales of all Marmon Group member companies neared $6.8 billion, with net earnings of more than $300 million.[2]

Together, Marmon companies operate more than five hundred facilities, including factories, distribution centers, and offices in fifty countries across six continents, and employ more than thirty-five thousand people.[3]

In 2001, *Forbes* magazine ranked The Marmon Group number nineteen on its list of the largest privately held companies in the United States.[4]

### The Pritzker Family

The Pritzker name has been prominent in America since the early twentieth century. In 1917, Nicholas Pritzker founded a successful law firm in Chicago. His sons, A. N.—Jay and Bob's father—Harry, and Jack, all joined the family business, then went on to build a fortune in real estate.

Jay Pritzker, A. N.'s eldest, followed his father's career path, receiving his law degree from Northwestern University in 1947. According to his younger brother Bob, Jay also inherited his father's intellect. "Jay was good at everything," Bob said of his late brother. "He was a remarkable guy. I've never known anybody who comes close to him. Every time they gave Jay an IQ test, he'd get the highest score."[5]

Bob, the middle son, was the only Pritzker who didn't pursue a law degree. Instead, he earned a degree in industrial engineering from the Illinois Institute of Technology in 1946. He also studied at

---

The brothers first bought the Colson Corporation, which they used to finance the purchase of Great American Industries (GAI) in 1955. Pictured above is the GAI logo.

the California Institute of Technology, the University of Illinois, the University of Zurich, and Case Institute of Technology.

Bob's decision to become an engineer was perhaps the driving force behind the creation of The Marmon Group. Raised in a family of lawyers and entrepreneurs, he was something of a mystery to his father. "My dad thought I went to engineering school because engineering was a good thing to take during the war," Bob Pritzker said. "That wasn't it at all. I really wanted to be a physicist."[6]

In college, however, Bob switched his focus from physics to engineering when he realized that he didn't have the natural ability to be "one of the greats" in the competitive world of physics. Instead, Bob began to develop a passion for management and mechanics. "When I was thinking, 'What kind of career do I want?' I always thought, 'Running a factory would be fun,'" Bob later said. "Every time I toured a factory, the more I saw it, the more I thought, 'That's for me.' There's enough science and mechanics and physics in it to satisfy my need for that, but there's more human contact, and I like people."[7]

A few years after he graduated, Bob landed a job at the Erie Manufacturing Company, which made automobile accessories. He proved himself a capable manager early on: by the age of twenty-four, he was already general manager of the company.

Bob's employment at Erie was cut short, however; he quit because of the company's contentious internal politics. After Erie, he worked as a consultant but found the work wasn't suited to his ambition. Then an opportunity presented itself.

"While I was doing that, my dad had a friend who had an interest in a company in Milwaukee that made paint rollers, and Dad and his partner had a chance to buy a bigger piece of it," Bob remembered.

*So Dad said, "Why don't you look into it?" One of the ways I looked into it was I asked everybody I knew, including Jay, if they knew anybody from another paint roller company. It turned out a lawyer friend of Jay's had a client who was in the paint roller business. So I called the guy, Stan Graham, and I said, "Could I come over to see you? I'd like to learn a little more about the paint roller business." He was a very nice guy, very outgoing. So I went over, and in the course of the conversation, he said, "If you want to be in the paint roller business, why don't you buy my company?"*[8]

Bob agreed, and he and Stan Graham formed a partnership to own and operate the paint roller business. Bob ran the company's manufacturing for about a year, functioning as the operational side of the partnership, while Stan Graham handled the sales. Then Jay intervened.

### The Colson Corporation

From early on, Bob Pritzker had misgivings about his partnership. Stan Graham was a good salesman but wasn't attuned to the operational side of the company, and his loose attention to costs made Bob nervous. Less than a year after paying twenty-six thousand dollars for his half of the partnership, Bob was approached by Jay with yet another opportunity. Jay had arranged for the purchase of a company called the Colson Corporation. Located in Elyria, Ohio, Colson manufactured a wide variety of products, including wheelchairs, bicycles, casters, and tricycles. In the early 1950s, Colson also produced 2.75-inch "Mighty Mouse" rockets for the U.S. Navy.

For Bob, Colson represented a considerable challenge. Not only was it much larger than either of the companies he had run so far, but the business had considerable problems. And, although his family was accustomed to buying and selling businesses and assets, this represented the first time a Pritzker would try to turn around an ailing manufacturing

Top: Bob Pritzker attended the Illinois Institute of Technology, where he earned a degree in industrial engineering. He is the only engineer in a family of lawyers.

Left: Jay Pritzker in 1942, during his stint as a naval aviator. Like his father, Jay Pritzker was an attorney, although he never practiced in the family firm.

The Worthington Manufacturing Company is visible in the background, identified by the words "Children's Fairy Machines." Fay Manufacturing became The Worthington Manufacturing Company in the 1890s after founder Winslow Fay sold his company. The name was later changed to the Colson Corporation. *(Photo courtesy Lorain County Historical Society.)*

company through the operational side. Finally, before he could even wade in, he had to extricate himself from the paint roller business.

"I had a college friend who was looking for something to do, so I asked him if he would like to buy my half interest," Bob remembered. "He said, 'Sure,' but my partner wouldn't accept him. So about three weeks later, my partner came to me and said, 'I think I'd like to move to California. Why don't we sell the whole company?' I ended up selling my half that I bought for $26,000 for about $2.5 million."[9]

Thus free of his partnership, Bob turned his whole attention to the Colson Corporation. Colson's antiquated manufacturing facility was a collection of connected buildings with assembly lines cutting through common walls. The oldest building dated from 1885, when the company was founded by Winslow L. Fay as The Fay Manufacturing Company. Fay's first products were a dirt scraper used to smooth the roads for cycling and an adult tricycle marketed under the "Fairy" brand name. A hand-powered tricycle was also produced, used primarily by the handicapped.[10]

After a series of initiatives, expansions, and name changes, the Colson Company was established in 1917. Its first products included three-wheeled, pedal-driven chairs, bicycles, wheelchairs, stretchers, dollies, carts, and a variety of parts for these items, primarily casters and wheels.[11]

Besides offering an opportunity for Bob, Colson was attractive because of its sheer potential. With its businesses and facilities in advanced disrepair, Colson had no room for anything but improvement, remembered Jay.

"The only reason owners of Colson and other troubled companies sold to us at bargain prices in the early days was because they had no place else to go," he remarked.[12]

But Jay had no desire to take advantage of the owners. Instead, he exploited a provision in the tax code to create a win-win situation. As Jack Steinberg wrote in his exacting history, *The Making of The Marmon Group*, Colson's owners wanted $30 a share.

*Colson had a book value of $42 a share. If [Jay] and Bob paid the going market price of $18 a share* *for its assets, the company could take a $24 loss on its books.*

*Earnings had been taxed at 50 percent in the recent profitable years. Under the law of the time, the company could recoup previously paid taxes over a three-year period to cover 50 percent—$12—of its $24-a-share loss. The stockholders would wind up with the $30 they were seeking; Jay and Bob would get Colson for little more than 40 percent of its book value. If they ran into serious difficulties they could sell or liquidate the company.*[13]

This method of financing, using the tax rebate, eventually became known as the "Pritzker method." To buy Colson, Jay ultimately worked out a deal in which Colson's stockholders received more than $3 million. A loan from the First National Bank

The Colson manufacturing plant in Elyria, Ohio, in the first decades of the 1900s, inset, and in the 1940s, below. From this large, inefficient, and sprawling plant, Colson produced a wide variety of products, including bicycles, casters, wheelchairs, and medical products.

of Chicago, based largely upon A. N. Pritzker's credit history, provided about 95 percent of the cash Jay and Bob needed. As Jay once remarked, "Because of Dad, I could get anything from the bank, even if the request was unreasonable."

**Running Colson**

On May 27, 1953, Jay Pritzker became chairman of the Colson Corporation and Bob Pritzker moved to Elyria as vice president for manufacturing. Bob immediately discovered that the company's difficulties ran far deeper than the brothers had even suspected. Before the Pritzkers bought the company, it had been led by Neely Powers, who was succeeded by Ed Glass around the time of the acquisition. Bob Pritzker would report to Glass.

"The place had more problems than I've ever seen," Bob remembered. "Every department was overinventoried. The turnover in the casters department was like 1.8 times a year. And the situation with the rockets was classic. They were supposed to ship twenty thousand a month, but they never got above four thousand a month, and we had one hundred thousand rejected rockets in inventory."[14]

Bob's first moves were to appoint a new foreman to handle rocket inspection and hire a former navy inspector to install a statistical quality control system. A few months later, production rose to the government contract–required twenty thousand rockets a month. In addition, the nearly one hundred thousand warehoused rocket assemblies were reworked to meet specifications. Colson realized nearly $1.5 million as it reduced its inventory of rejected rockets, enough to pay off the purchase price and provide some much-needed working capital.

Bob's next task was to get out of the bicycle business. Though Colson bicycles and tricycles were at one time among the best selling in the country, the competition from foreign makers grew intense in the early 1950s. "Colson's cost for a twenty-six-inch bike at the factory was $30.50," Bob said. "However, we could buy an exact duplicate in Germany, just as good quality, delivered to our dock, freight and duty paid, for $23.50."[15]

The Colson bike line was sold to a firm that produced its own line of juvenile vehicles, Evans Products, based in Plymouth, Michigan. After the

Ronald Reagan and Dorothy Malone ride a Colson bike on the set of *Law and Order*. Colson bikes were competitive until the 1950s, when cheaper foreign imports eroded their market share.

sale, the bikes were labeled as "Evans-Colson" for a couple of years, and then just "Evans."[16]

After these early initiatives, Colson was in better operating shape than it had been in years, and on January 1, 1954, Glass retired and Bob "inherited the presidency by default."[17] Although Colson was greatly improved, its future remained uncertain. With the bike division gone, so was more than 25 percent of the company's total sales volume. Profits came from the caster line and from rockets produced under semiannual government contracts, which could be canceled at any time.

While the removal of the bicycle division liberated badly needed production space, the antiquated factory and the wheelchair division continued to be plagued with problems. Bob didn't want to produce wheelchairs, so he later sold the manufacturing operation to Cort Shea, a Colson employee, with a ten-year agreement that Shea would continue to make wheelchairs under the Colson nameplate, in addition to his own brand. Then, at Shea's request, Bob hired a salesman to specialize in Colson wheelchairs. Shortly before the ten years was up, Shea recruited the salesman and went off on his own. Over the years, the former wheelchair division of

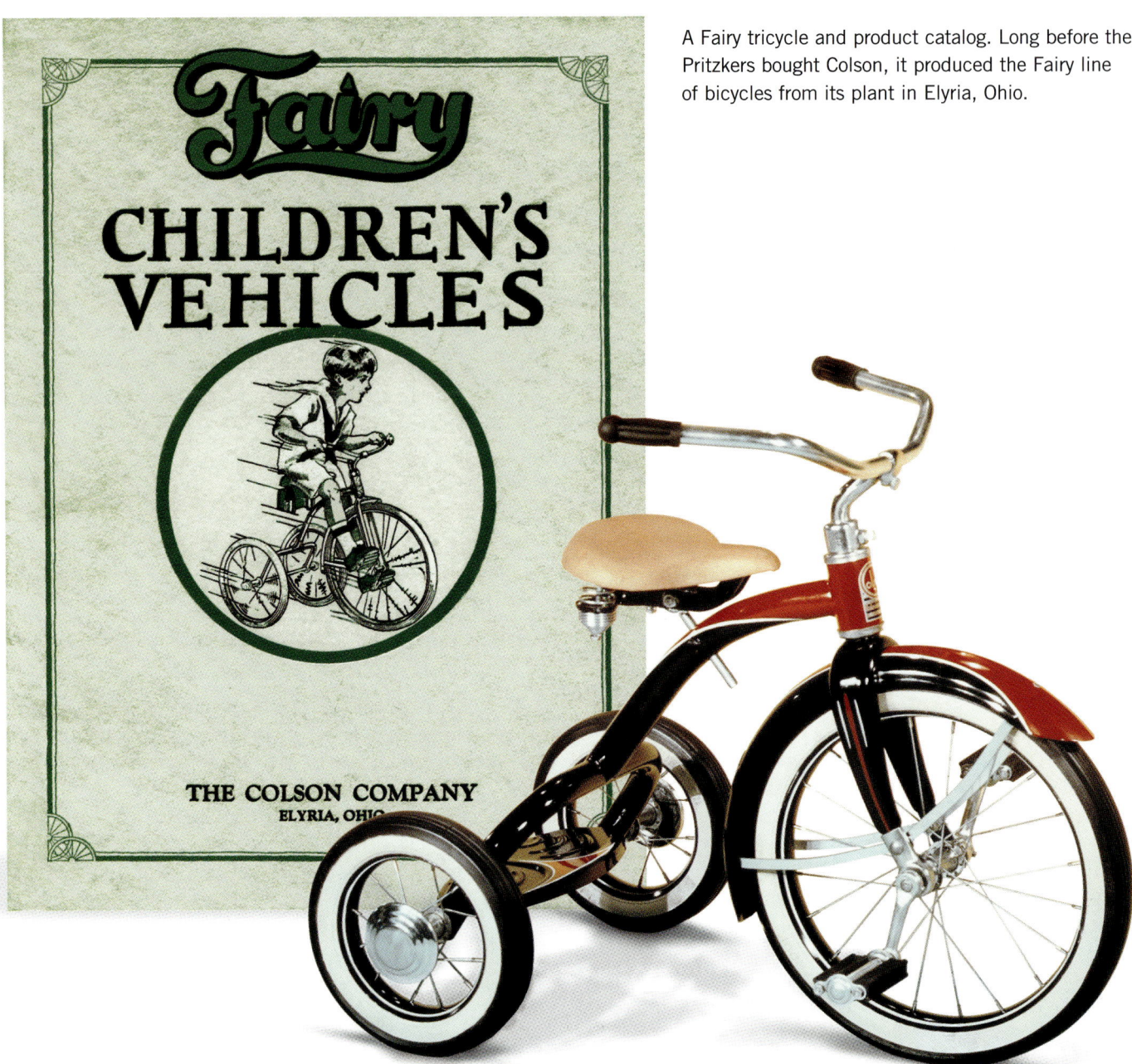

A Fairy tricycle and product catalog. Long before the Pritzkers bought Colson, it produced the Fairy line of bicycles from its plant in Elyria, Ohio.

the Colson Corporation would evolve into Invacare Corporation, the world's largest wheelchair manufacturer. "It taught me a lesson," Bob later remarked. "I was done in by one of my own people."[18]

The situation at the Colson plant continued to pose challenges. Labor relations at the plant were difficult, to say the least. The effects of a disastrous seven-week strike during the summer of 1952 (the first strike in the company's history) continued to linger.[19] For example, even after the bicycle business was divested, union officials refused Bob's commonsense request to modify vacation schedules that had originally been designed to accommodate the seasonal peaks and slumps in bicycle production.

**Service Caster & Truck Acquisition**

Given the unstable atmosphere, Jay set out to find a product line that would replace the bikes and enhance Colson's prospects. He settled upon the Service Caster & Truck Company of Albion,

Michigan, after Arthur Green, a friend of his father's who was in the commercial loan business, suggested the struggling firm might be available.

The firm made products that complemented Colson's: medium- and heavy-duty casters that carried loads of up to four hundred pounds. Colson's caster line maxed out at three hundred pounds. Combining the lines would give Colson the broadest range of casters in the industry. Service also manufactured a line of mechanical and electrohydraulic lifting equipment at its twenty-three-thousand-square-foot plant in Somerville, Massachusetts. Most importantly, Service Caster & Truck met the criteria for Jay's tax rebate maneuver.[20]

The firm's net worth was $1 million. Its owners wanted $600,000. During the Korean War, when the company held a lucrative U.S. Navy contract to produce gasoline-powered forklift trucks, Service had paid far more than the owner's asking price in excess profit taxes, which ran to more than 70 percent during the war. Jay mapped a way through the maze:

*If we paid nothing for the business and they took a million-dollar loss, they would get back more in tax refunds than they were asking for the business.*

*I said to myself, 'You can't pay nothing. The IRS will come after you like a herd.' So we paid a nominal*

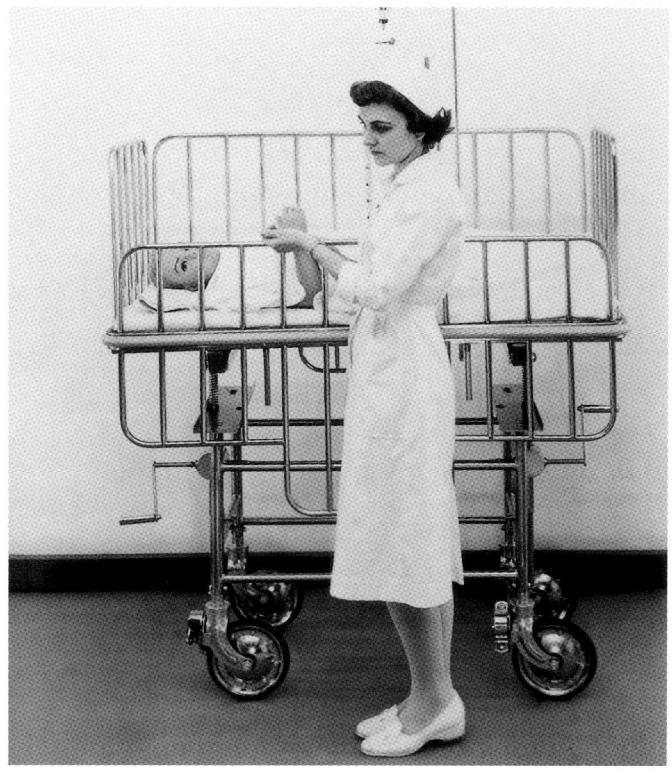

Above and below: Colson included a line of wheelchairs and other medical products. Shortly after the acquisition, as part of his effort to streamline Colson, Bob Pritzker sold the manufacturing operation to an employee. Eventually, the wheelchair division broke away and grew into today's hospital-products giant Invacare Corporation.

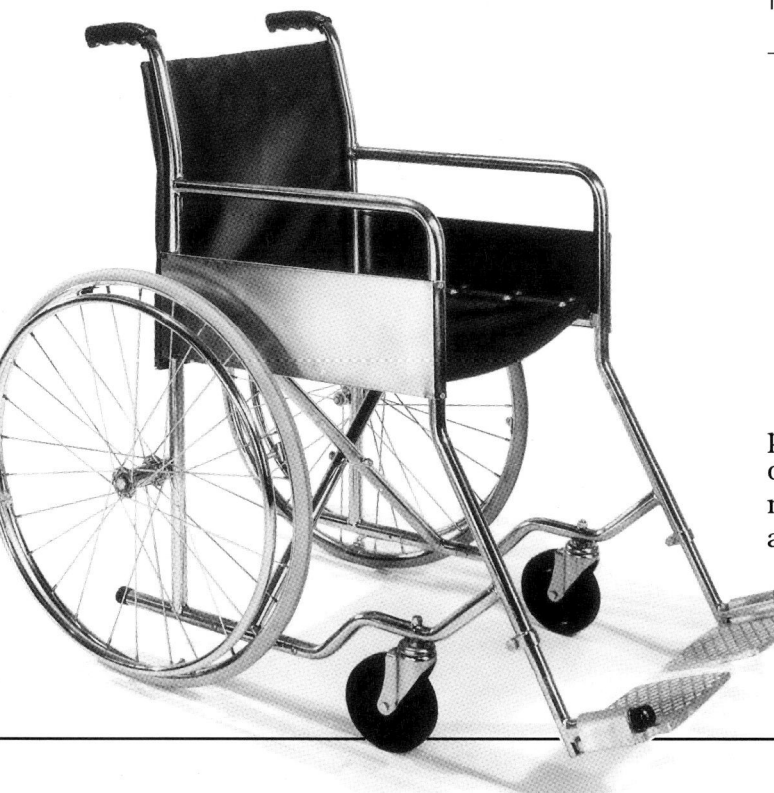

*amount, something like $150,000, for the assets, and we structured the deal to make it tax efficient. That meant selling the accounts receivable to a third party at book value and placing inventory on a last-in/first-out basis to avoid quick realization of income. The assets were bought separately by a Pritzker trust.*[21]

After the acquisition, Bob combined the best products and people from both companies. He dropped the Service name and merged its caster and material-handling equipment (hand trucks, dollies, and platform trucks) with Colson's.

In May 1954, Colson broke ground on a forty-four-acre site in Elyria for a single-story, forty-thousand-square-foot production plant in which the manufacture of the material-handling

Right: In 1954, hoping to make the manufacturing process more efficient, Bob Pritzker broke ground for a new factory in Elyria, Ohio. This plant would produce only hand trucks and other material-handling equipment. It was eventually divested.

Below: The jewel in the Colson crown was its line of casters. Bob, as an engineer, had developed an affinity for casters and, with his brother's help, sought to develop or acquire the country's most complete line. Pictured are some of Colson's original casters and hand trucks, circa 1950.

equipment could be consolidated. In Canada, after considerable study of local markets, Bob severed company ties with a long-standing distributor and in September 1954 formed a wholly owned Toronto subsidiary, Colson (Canada) Limited, to handle sales, distribution, and assembly of Colson's products in Canada.

Outwardly, Colson was beginning to look better than ever. Bob even formed a new division, Colson Medical Instruments, whose products included blood pressure monitoring and recording instruments. The new hand-truck plant was completed, and there were plans for five more 40,000-square-foot incremental additions over the next several years to replace the current factory with a modern 240,000-square-foot facility. Inwardly, however, Bob and Jay knew Colson was still in trouble. Its labor difficulties continued, and it had assumed additional debt. Also, projected pretax earnings seemed unlikely to provide for more than its basic survival, let alone construction of a much-needed new plant.

"We had to move but couldn't afford to," Bob said. "Sooner or later we'd be bankrupt, and that would be the worst thing that could happen. We couldn't default on our loans. My career was at stake. Would anybody ever count on me again? We couldn't ask the family to bail us out. We were raised to be independent and responsible."[22]

Bob and Jay concluded there was only one way out: merge Colson with another company that had sufficient working capital to finance a new plant.

### Great American Industries

In May 1955, the Pritzkers agreed to sell Colson to Great American Industries, Inc. (GAI), a publicly traded company based in Meriden, Connecticut. Though founded in 1942 as an association of nine other firms, whose product lines ran the gamut from fire trucks to beauty products,

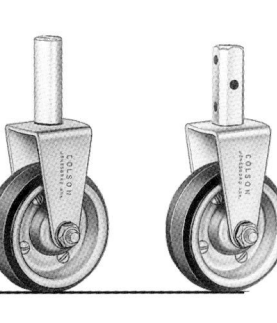

GAI had shrunk to just two operations during the postwar years.

The first, Connecticut Telephone & Electric, produced intercom systems for industry and field telephones for the U.S. Army Signal Corps. The second company, Rubatex, manufactured a range of closed-cell sponge-rubber products used in sporting equipment, automobiles, and railroad cars.

Under the deal negotiated with GAI president Robert T. Dunlap, the Pritzkers became GAI's largest shareholders—obtaining 437,500 shares worth $1.75 million plus a note for $250,000. Bob was to remain Colson's president.

To limit the Pritzker brothers' voting power, however, their 26 percent stake in GAI was put into a voting trust whose trustees represented both GAI management and the Pritzkers. The shares couldn't be voted by the brothers alone, who held certificates in the trust, not the stock directly. The agreement, however, allowed the Pritzkers to sell their shares at any time, thereby leaving the trust.

As it turned out, it was a contract stipulation that Jay needed to employ on June 28, 1955, the very day he and Bob were to be elected to the GAI board of directors. According to Steinberg's company history, when Bob and Jay arrived at GAI's Meriden headquarters for the 11:00 A.M. meeting, they were asked to wait in an office located some distance from the company's boardroom.[23]

"We were a couple of naive, apple-cheeked kids from Chicago," Jay explained. "We sat in that office and waited. And waited. A couple of hours went by, and we began to wonder what was going on. At last we were ushered in to meet the other directors, who looked to us like Boston Brahmins. One of the nonmanagement directors slipped me a piece of paper. On it was one word: 'Fight!' Fight? I think, Fight what?"

Jay soon found out. Board chairman and company president Dunlap revealed that the directors had just resolved to purchase an aviation supply and service firm, Air Associates, Inc., of Teterboro, New Jersey, for an amount of stock similar to that paid for Colson.

"Dunlap obviously wanted countervailing power to maintain management's hold," explained Jay. "With Air Associates in the picture, we would lose our nominal control of GAI. We would have given up Colson just to become two of twelve directors."

But the Pritzkers would not allow themselves to be so easily outmaneuvered. During the board's lunch break, Jay telephoned his father back in Chicago for help with an emergency plan. "Dad, right now, call Art Green," he said. "Sell him our stock in Great American Industries for four dollars a share and get 10 percent down to legitimatize the deal."

# THE PRITZKER FAMILY

WHEN JACOB N. PRITZKER FIRST arrived in Chicago from Kiev in 1881 with his ten-year-old son, Nicholas, the impoverished Russian immigrant couldn't even afford to buy his son a coat. When he took the young boy to the city's Michael Reese Hospital to be treated for a severe cold, the hospital bought him one for nine dollars.

"It was the best investment they ever made," Nicholas's son, A. N. Pritzker, once said. "I paid them back for that coat—about a million times."[1]

Not much information exists about Jacob N. Pritzker, though an 1886 Chicago directory listed his business as "trimmings" and gave his address as "554 State."[2]

His son Nicholas, born in Kiev on July 19, 1871, is regarded as founder of the family's considerable fortune. Nicholas began his career as a newspaper boy and bootjack.[3] With Russian and German dictionaries as his constant companions, he taught himself to read and write English. After the arrival of his mother, Sophia (Schwartzman), from Kiev,[4] Nicholas worked at a succession of jobs and graduated from high school.

He continued his formal education and in 1888, when only seventeen years old, became a druggist.[5] On March 4, 1891, a few months before his twentieth birthday, he married Anna Cohn. Throughout Nicholas's early career, his father wanted him to be a rabbi. But Nicholas was more interested in the law and resumed his studies at Northwestern University in 1892. Ten years later he graduated from DePaul University with his law degree.

"My grandfather was very serious about being a lawyer," remembered Bob Pritzker. "If he

Nicholas Pritzker immigrated to America when he was ten years old and later founded the Pritzker family law practice.

After their lunch, Jay addressed the board: "Gentlemen, we have sold our stock in Great American. There no longer is a voting trust. The new owner will vigorously oppose the acquisition of Air Associates."

The Air Associates deal was effectively dead. At the next GAI board meeting, on July 28, it was officially buried. But a new, five-member Executive Finance Committee, charged with reviewing all proposed mergers, acquisitions, and sales, was born. Both "apple-cheeked kids from Chicago" were appointed. Moreover, Dunlap resigned as board chairman and was replaced by Jay.[24]

### Troubles at Contelco

Upon his return to Elyria, Bob learned the navy was soliciting bids to produce launchers for the Mighty Mouse rockets Colson was already making. His staff wanted to go after the launcher contract as didn't think the argument was appropriate, he wouldn't take the case."[6]

In 1917, Nicholas Pritzker established his private practice, Pritzker & Pritzker. During these years, Nicholas and Anna had three sons, A. N. (Abram), Harry, and Jack. All three attended college and law school and followed their father into the practice of law.

Harry, the eldest, died in 1957, the same year as Nicholas. He had become a criminal lawyer who had little connection to the family business. He was also considered something of a raconteur and once considered going into vaudeville.[7] Jack, the youngest, passed away in 1979. He had been the family law firm's real estate expert.

Jay and Bob's father, A. N., the middle child, who died in 1986, was a deal-maker and gifted intellectual. "He was entrepreneurial down to his toenails," remembered Bob. "He was the best at arithmetic I had ever encountered. I saw him add a column of seven-digit numbers while he was having a fight about a legal issue over the telephone. He slept about five hours a night, and the other nineteen, his mind was going a mile a minute."[8]

A. N. also had three sons. Jay, the eldest, was also a lawyer. In addition to his role in The Marmon Group, Jay led the family-owned Hyatt hotels until his death in 1999 at age 76. Donald, the youngest child, was a lawyer and became president of Hyatt until he suffered a fatal heart attack in 1972 at age 39. In an unusual move for a Pritzker, the middle son, Bob, pursued a degree in engineering and cofounded and became president of The Marmon Group.

Over the generations, the Pritzker family has built up a large group of holdings. The majority of the family's interests are privately held by numerous trusts, the oldest of which was set up in the 1930s by A. N. Pritzker.[9] With few exceptions, family assets reside in privately held companies, joint ventures, and partnerships that release little financial information. The family, whose holdings once included *McCall's* magazine and Braniff Airlines, now owns Hyatt Hotels & Resorts, a controlling interest in Royal Caribbean Cruise Line, and real estate holdings.[10]

Toward the end of his life, Nicholas Pritzker wrote a small book that has never been published but is passed down from Pritzker to Pritzker. Its theme: Your only immortality is the impact you have on your successors.[11] Most would agree that Nicholas lives on.

---

well but had been delayed because some fifty companies were considering bids and the navy had run out of sets of specifications.

Not everyone wanted the business, however. The current manufacturer of the launchers, located by sheer coincidence in the same building as Bob's paint roller company, had decided not to seek renewal of the contract. As Bob pointed out, "Any time the company that was making it already was preparing to turn the contract down, you knew that meant something."[25]

Given the competition, when Bob's people told him they had decided on a bid of $28.95 per launcher, he told them, "Guys, don't hold your breath. With that many bidders, if $28.95 is the right price, some idiot is sure to make a mistake and bid $19.50."

Some weeks later, Bob was shocked to discover "some idiot" had in fact bid $19.50: a sister company, Connecticut Telephone & Electric (Contelco). Determined to get to the bottom of the affair, Bob and two of his employees went to Meriden to examine Contelco's proposal. They were further amazed to discover that Contelco had submitted its bid without even looking at the specification sheets. The material costs alone were greater than $19.50 per launcher, not to mention that Contelco had no experience with that kind of product.[26] Bob estimated that Contelco would lose $5.50 on every rocket launcher it produced at that cost.

Worse yet, he became suspicious. If Contelco was willing to make such a wild bid on this project, were there other cases like it? To his horror, Bob found that "every contract we looked at was the same way. They were losers before they opened the box."[27]

Bob, now "not a happy camper,"[28] reported his findings in a letter to GAI's board. Dunlap countered with a positive report on GAI operations and called for approval of a proposed Contelco plant expansion. The board, however, was shaky. In November 1955, during a special board meeting,

Bob was named the new president of Connecticut Telephone & Electric while Dunlap remained president of GAI.²⁹

Bob spent the next two months investigating Contelco's business practices. What he discovered was far worse than a pattern of chronic underbidding. But he also knew that Contelco was being protected by Dunlap and by its own auditors, meaning he would need an airtight case for the board of directors. This turned out to be fairly easy. He asked each board member to tour the factory with an employee guide. During their tours, he invited them to randomly select pieces of inventory, and the guide would tell them what that inventory was used for or if it was obsolete. Jay Pritzker was one of the board members who took the tour, and every piece of inventory he identified was obsolete.

In January 1956, after two months of investigation, Bob was ready to make a formal presentation to the board. Minutes of that board meeting reflect the events that took place.

---

The Great American Industries acquisition did not go as smoothly as planned. One of the company's divisions, Connecticut Telephone, was discovered to be keeping fraudulent inventory records. The Pritzkers sued, alleging that they had been duped into paying too much for GAI.

*The Chairman (Jay) then discussed Connecticut's inventory. He said that he was convinced, as were his brother and independent persons who had inspected the company's plant recently, that the inventory was heavily overvalued, excessive, and to a great degree worthless.*³⁰

Of the $2.6 million of inventory on Contelco's books, a sum certified by the firm's independent auditors, Bob estimated that more than $1.5 million was worthless. For example, obsolete hospital nurses' call systems that had not been made for a decade and were no longer even being marketed were never written off. Instead, they were valued at original cost and kept on the books. Indeed, when Bob offered the call systems on a consignment basis to a business friend in Cleveland, Ohio, the friend "stated that it would not pay him to make room in his plant for these items since they were completely unsaleable and outdated."³¹

The effects of the inflated company assets were considerable. Not only had stockholders obviously been cheated, but taxes and executive bonuses had been paid on phantom earnings. Bob and Jay, the firm's largest stockholders, calculated they received one hundred thousand fewer shares of GAI stock for Colson than they should have.³²

As Jay told the board during the January 11 meeting, Contelco was nearly bankrupt. He pointed

out that with debts of $1.7 million, including $585,000 in loans owed to or guaranteed by GAI, and with cash and receivables of only $500,000, the company could not pay its bills. Consequently, suppliers refused to ship the new tools and materials needed to meet government contracts, which were the lion's share of its business.

Jay suggested selling the firm for as little as $250,000 to anyone who would assume its liabilities and fulfill its contracts. He added that Bob thought even $250,000 might be too high an asking price, but the Pritzkers had some bank obligations that they wanted to pay off.

Two weeks later, Dunlap and two other executives sent Jay a fifteen-page letter accusing the Pritzker brothers of willfully trying to destroy Contelco and liquidate it in order to gain control of GAI. They defended their management and called for the continued operation of Contelco, as well as its expansion.

At a meeting held in Meriden the following week to decide the fate of Contelco, Norman Price, the former head of Colson's bike division, joined Bob and Jay on the board, giving them numerical parity with Dunlap's management faction. The outside board members held the balance of power.

Jay announced that he and Bob were more convinced than ever that Contelco needed to be disposed of at any price. Additional research into the government contracts revealed the firm would lose money on many of them, he said.

It didn't take long for Jay's argument to prevail on three of the outside board members, who by the February 9 board meeting were convinced that Contelco was seriously troubled. With the outside directors decidedly against them, Dunlap and his supporters resigned. Bob was then elected president of Great American Industries.

One of Colson's biggest pieces of business at the time of the Pritzker acquisition was a navy contract to produce the Mighty Mouse rocket. Unfortunately, production was so inefficient and error prone that the company had thousands of rejected rockets sitting in inventory.

Not long thereafter, Connecticut Telephone & Electric was sold to a Boston-based manufacturer of bus door openers. The deal produced federal tax-loss credits that offset $405,310 earned on sales of $13.5 million in 1955 and gave GAI substantial carryovers for 1956 and much of 1957.[33]

As Bob later explained in a letter to shareholders, a major step toward lowering operating costs was also taken. "This cut home office expenses, since the corporate home was moved from Meriden, Connecticut, to quarters made available to it in Colson's main plant at Elyria, Ohio. The home office staff has been cut from nine to four persons. In each position, the salary of the present executive is lower than that of his former counterpart."[34]

The cost-cutting measures proved necessary. Even though struggling Colson was rewarded for its rocket production improvements with a new, six-month, $850,000 government contract—during which the one millionth rocket manufactured by Colson came off the line—sales at the Rubatex division suffered a sharp decline. Auto production and sales in the United States had fallen dramatically during 1956, and because the auto industry was the greatest user of Rubatex's foam rubber products, GAI's earnings were hit hard.

**Colson Strikes**

In mid-August 1956, another challenge arose. The labor situation at Colson finally boiled over, and its union called for a general strike.[35] "It was absurd," Bob said. "I didn't know what they wanted. They walked out before we had a meeting, so there was no way to settle it beforehand."

"The strike was a crushing blow to Bob," Jay added. "He took it very personally. He had worked with the union and regarded the employees as his friends. He had tried hard to make things work."

Three weeks into the strike, at a September 5 board meeting, the Pritzkers laid out three options that Bob had developed: sell Colson, liquidate it, or move it out of Elyria, where confrontational labor relations seemed to prevail.

Above and right: Great American Industries' other division, Rubatex, was a major earner until the late 1950s, when a downturn in the auto industry hit its core market for foam rubber products.

At the time of this presentation, the Pritzkers themselves didn't have any real preference—until a 3 A.M. labor negotiation broke down and Bob declared, "I can't deal with this."[36]

The board authorized Bob to move to any location he deemed fit, and the strike was settled on terms favorable to the union with the stipulation that the Pritzkers had the right to close or move the plant if they deemed it necessary.

Bob immediately began looking for a new location. Before long, he found a town he liked in Arkansas—but was politely informed by the town leaders that "they didn't want us." Instead, they referred him to the town of Jonesboro, also in Arkansas.[37]

There were definite advantages to relocating in Arkansas. Under a program offered by the recently formed Arkansas Industrial Development Commission, companies operating in high-cost northeastern states were being offered low-cost construction loans, employee training, and tax abatements to move to Arkansas. Consequently, in March 1957, Bob asked the board for permission to move Colson's caster division and some lift-jack and skid production to a new plant he proposed to build in Jonesboro.

"We got there by mistake," Bob later said. "We didn't know it was the best place to run a factory."[38]

Due to planned technological advances in the Mighty Mouse rocket, Bob thought it prudent not to compete for any future rocket contracts. On Jay's motion, the board approved the move and asked Bob to sell Colson's lift-equipment division in Somerville, Massachusetts, and its truck operation in Elyria.

That summer, with construction under way on Colson's new eighty-nine-thousand-square-foot plant in Jonesboro, Bob began to pare down the firm. The medical products unit was sold to its general manager, but buyers for Elyria's truck line and the lift-equipment plant in Somerville couldn't be found. The division was spared, however, when several sizable new orders made the plant profitable again.

Even throughout all this pruning, the union members refused to believe that Bob was actually planning to move the company.

*The day the machines [left for] Jonesboro, one of the foremen came up and said, "Bob, you're not going to believe this, but we've loaded up the last truck and I was pretty sad. This thing is moving out of town and my dad worked here. So I said to the union guys that were with me, 'Come on, let's have a cup of coffee.' I guess I showed my depression because one of the guys said, 'Don't worry. Bob Pritzker is a pretty clever guy. He's got these trucks all lined up down the road about ten miles, and when we give in for everything, he'll turn around and bring them back.' "*[39]

### The Move to Jonesboro

On October 11, 1957, with two hundred new employees and an efficient new factory, production officially began at Colson's new Jonesboro plant. During 1958, its first full year of operation, the new facility nearly broke even on sales of $2.7 million.

Nevertheless, with Rubatex struggling and with Colson in constant need of operating capital, GAI was still in trouble. That made it a suitable target for Walter S. Mack, a sixty-three-year-old takeover specialist, best known as the former chairman of United Cigar-Whelan Stores, a drugstore chain. Mack had also served as chairman and president of Pepsi Cola in the late 1940s.

His National Phoenix Industries was a holding company that included beverage canning, rubber products, and hand power tool manufacturers. But because of losses suffered by nearly all of National's operations in 1956, Mack's own position was fragile.

That, however, didn't stop him from attempting acquisitions he could pay for with National stock, and on July 17, 1958, Bob and Jay agreed to sell their controlling interest in GAI to National for approximately $1.9 million in notes, some $1.5 million of it secured by GAI stock, the rest unsecured. If Mack were to default on the quarterly payments, Bob and Jay's stock was to be returned and the notes canceled.[40]

"My own feeling," Jay said, "was we'd get Colson back. Walter Mack was very likable, but I wasn't sure he'd follow through on his commitments."

In August, Mack replaced Jay as chairman of both GAI and Colson. Bob resigned his presidencies, returned to Chicago, and set up an office near Jay's in the Pritzker law firm.

With the other businesses sold, Jay began to negotiate the purchase of a farm and animal husbandry equipment manufacturer called the James Mfg. Co. in Fort Atkinson, Wisconsin. Bob prepared himself to manage the facility when the deal was closed.

In November, however, Jay's prudence paid off when National Phoenix missed the payments on the notes given to Bob and Jay for their GAI stock.

Consequently, Colson was returned to the Pritzkers in exchange for their GAI stock and their agreement to drop their unsettled claim for one hundred thousand additional shares in consequence of Contelco's inventory fraud. Bob and Jay also agreed to reimburse GAI $200,000 over a ten-year period for a portion of the nearly $1.4 million in working capital Colson had received.[41] This money had been used to relocate Colson to Arkansas. Ultimately, although the Pritzkers lost a small amount of money in these dealings, the freedom to move Colson more than made up for the loss.

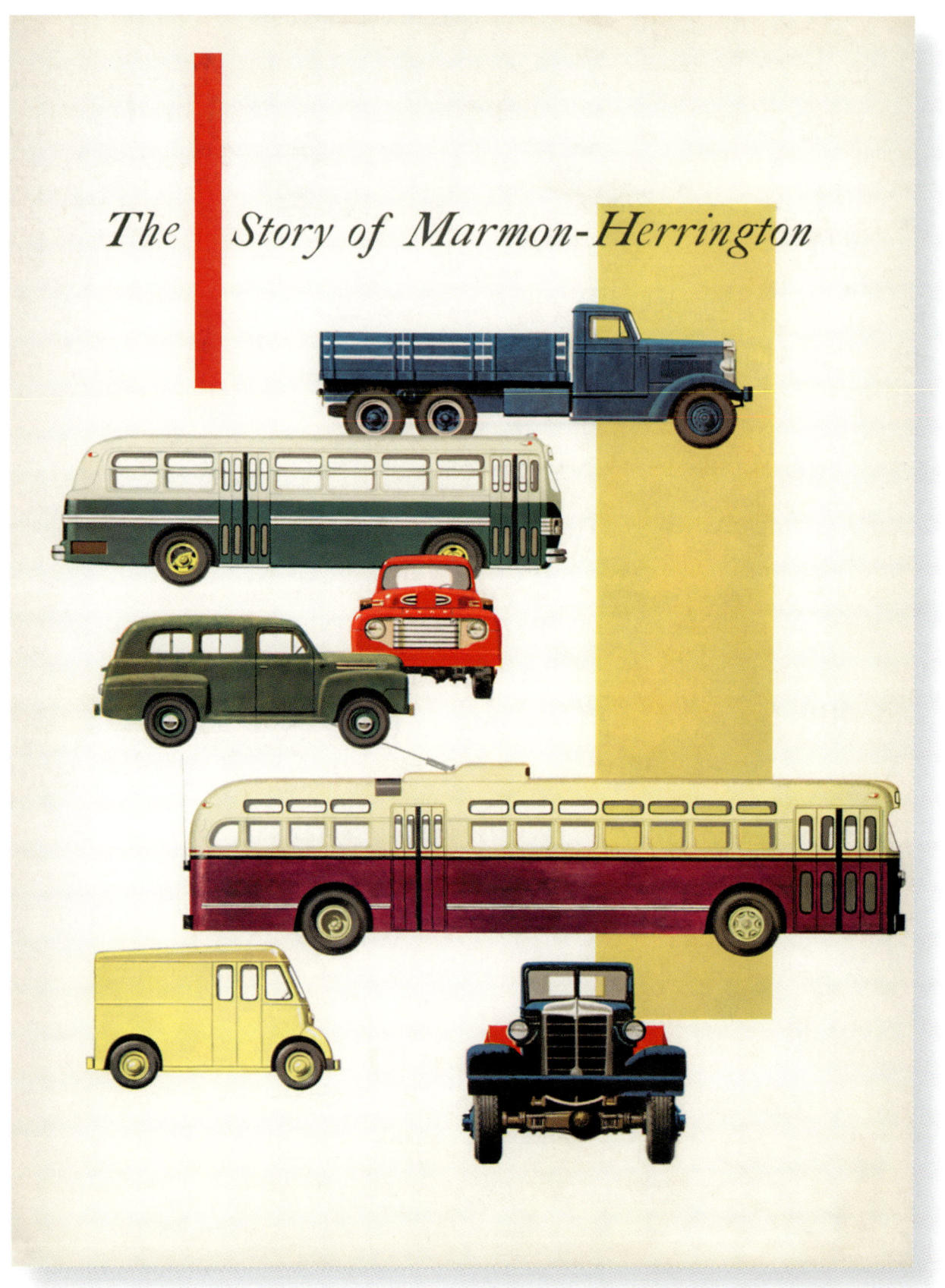

In 1962, the Pritzker brothers bought Marmon-Herrington, whose range of businesses included four-wheel-drive conversion kits.

CHAPTER TWO

# THE MARMON GROUP IS BORN

## 1959–1964

*The word "Group" was rarely used in those days. I chose it because I didn't want to create a monolithic entity. I wanted to make it clear that ours was a group of companies, not a corporation with a bunch of divisions.*

—Bob Pritzker, explaining the name of The Marmon Group

IN CONTROL OF COLSON once again, Bob and Jay Pritzker began to look for more companies to acquire. Over the next five years, the brothers would rapidly expand their holdings to encompass a wide variety of manufacturing companies. There were several reasons behind this game plan. One was simply ambition: the Pritzker brothers were a very effective team, able to creatively finance and then restructure an ailing manufacturing company. Another was diversification. They understood that a broad-based organization with manufacturing operations in a variety of industries would be protected during normal economic swings.

### James Mfg. Co.

In the fall of 1958, the brothers targeted the James Mfg. Co. in Fort Atkinson, Wisconsin. Typical of many of Bob and Jay's early acquisitions, James was in trouble.

Founded in 1906, it produced ventilation, feeding, and cleaning systems under the name Jamesway for dairy barns and poultry houses. It also had a small foundry that made iron castings and pipe fittings for assembly and installation.[1] The market for farm products had fallen sharply during the 1950s.

The acquisition closed in January 1959, and Bob moved quickly to revitalize the business. He first promoted Chester A. Hanson from sales vice president to general manager. Then he converted the company's money-losing foundry into a separate business, the James Foundry Corporation. With a new general manager in place, it grew to occupy eighty thousand square feet in the Fort Atkinson main plant and eventually supported a workforce of 113. To help the ever dwindling number of small family farmers purchase Jamesway products, the Pritzkers next set up the Atkinson Finance Company and bought another finance company called the Farm Equipment Acceptance Corporation.

On the manufacturing side, under Bob's direction the company instituted new product-design, inventory, and cost-control measures, hoping to reduce inventory. This measure was so successful that by the end of the year, James's standing inventory had been reduced by $751,000—a sum that accounted for nearly all of the company's earnings that year. In 1960, the company shaved $673,000 more off the inventories. Combined, the reductions recouped nearly all of the $1.4 million the Pritzkers had paid for the firm.[2]

Among the redesigned products, the firm's poultry incubator-hatcher house stood out, although the

---

The logo that appeared on the 1957 Jamesway annual report. Jay bought Jamesway two years later. Bob revitalized the company and introduced an innovative poultry feeder.

The Big J poultry incubator changed the business of poultry farming. Using this tightly controlled mechanical hatchery, farms could produce twelve thousand chicks every three days.

company continued to make animal husbandry products also.

Called the Jamesway "Big J," this mechanized feeding, watering, cleaning, and ventilation system could produce twelve thousand chicks every three days—four times the output of the equipment marketed by James's competitors.

To further offset the effects of the shrinking U.S. farm market, in September 1960 another Pritzker family firm purchased Graham Metal Products Company in Preston, Ontario. Graham manufactured small poultry feeders and brooders as well as other livestock equipment and gas ranges for the Canadian market. Bob sold off the nonpoultry product lines and established a unit in Preston called Jamesway Company Limited to make and market both Jamesway and Graham products in Canada. A new company, N.V. Jamesway, had already been started in 1959 in the Netherlands to give James a presence in Europe. Also that year, to market both Colson and Jamesway products in Central and South America, Bob had established Associated Manufacturers International S.A. (AMISA), a Panama-based firm.

Bob oversaw these growing operations from Chicago, frequently traveling to both the James and the Colson operations.

In 1959, he hired a new manager to run Colson's operations in Arkansas. George Jones was recruited from General Steelwares to run the new caster plant. It was the beginning of a twenty-seven-year career working with Bob Pritzker.

"I took a look at the plant down there and I knew I could do a lot with it," Jones said. "It wasn't in very good shape. We turned it around inside of a year."[3]

## L. A. Darling

The Pritzkers' main focus, however, was more growth. Throughout 1959 and 1960, the brothers successfully negotiated the purchase of L. A. Darling Company.

Darling had been founded in 1897 by August Visel as the Ideal Fixture Company, then purchased by Lewis Archer Darling in the early part of the twentieth century and renamed.[4] Its largest and most profitable business unit designed and manufactured retail-store merchandising equipment in a two-hundred-thousand-square-foot plant in Bronson, Michigan. The company's main product was called Viz-U-Sell, a vertical steel stand that held adjustable shelf brackets. The system had long been favored by such retail leaders as J. C. Penney.[5]

"There were two virtues to Viz-U-Sell," Bob Pritzker later said. "One was that it was infinitely variable, and two was that less was exposed so the product display was more attractive."[6]

A 1961 company brochure described Darling's vision.

> [L. A. Darling] sensed the swing to self-service merchandising in the 1940s in the department store and variety store field by marketing the first complete line of metal store fixtures, a line which very shortly removed the cabinet maker and his wooden cabinets and shelving from the merchandising scene. Since then the company has taken the merchandising slogan "show more, sell more" as a design dictum.[7]

Darling had three additional divisions in nearby Coldwater. The Workwall Division made movable partitions and paneling for business offices, industrial plants, hospitals, laboratories, and schools in a sixty-thousand-square-foot plant. The Plastic Division, which occupied a separate, fifty-thousand-square-foot facility, specialized in the promannequins. A third unit, the Midwest Foundry Company, produced grey iron and steel castings for Darling's own products, as well as for outside customers, in an eighty-thousand-square-foot plant.[8]

"Bob and I looked at [Darling] and concluded the foundry looked like a good business, but the store fixture business was questionable," explained Jay.[9]

In 1959, the Pritzkers bought 24.38 percent of L. A. Darling stock from the estate of Trowbridge Stanley, the firm's recently deceased president of twenty-nine years. Soon after the initial purchase, they offered to exchange their Colson Corporation stock for 125,000 additional shares—a deal that virtually mirrored the one that gave them control of Great American Industries five years earlier. In addition, the Pritzkers offered to purchase an additional 30,000 shares for $16 a share.

Darling's shareholders approved the stock swap, and Colson became a wholly owned subsidiary of L. A. Darling. The Pritzkers' stake in Darling increased to 43.27 percent.[10] Bob relayed the news to Colson employees in a letter dated May 16, 1960:

> I am pleased to announce that The Colson Corporation has become affiliated with the L. A. Darling Company of Bronson, Michigan, through an exchange of stock. All employees and executives of The Colson Corporation will remain in their present

A copy of the L. A. Darling logo from the 1951 annual report. To assume control of the company, the Pritzkers used familiar tactics. They swapped shares in their Colson Corporation for a controlling interest in L. A. Darling, revitalized the company, and eventually took it private.

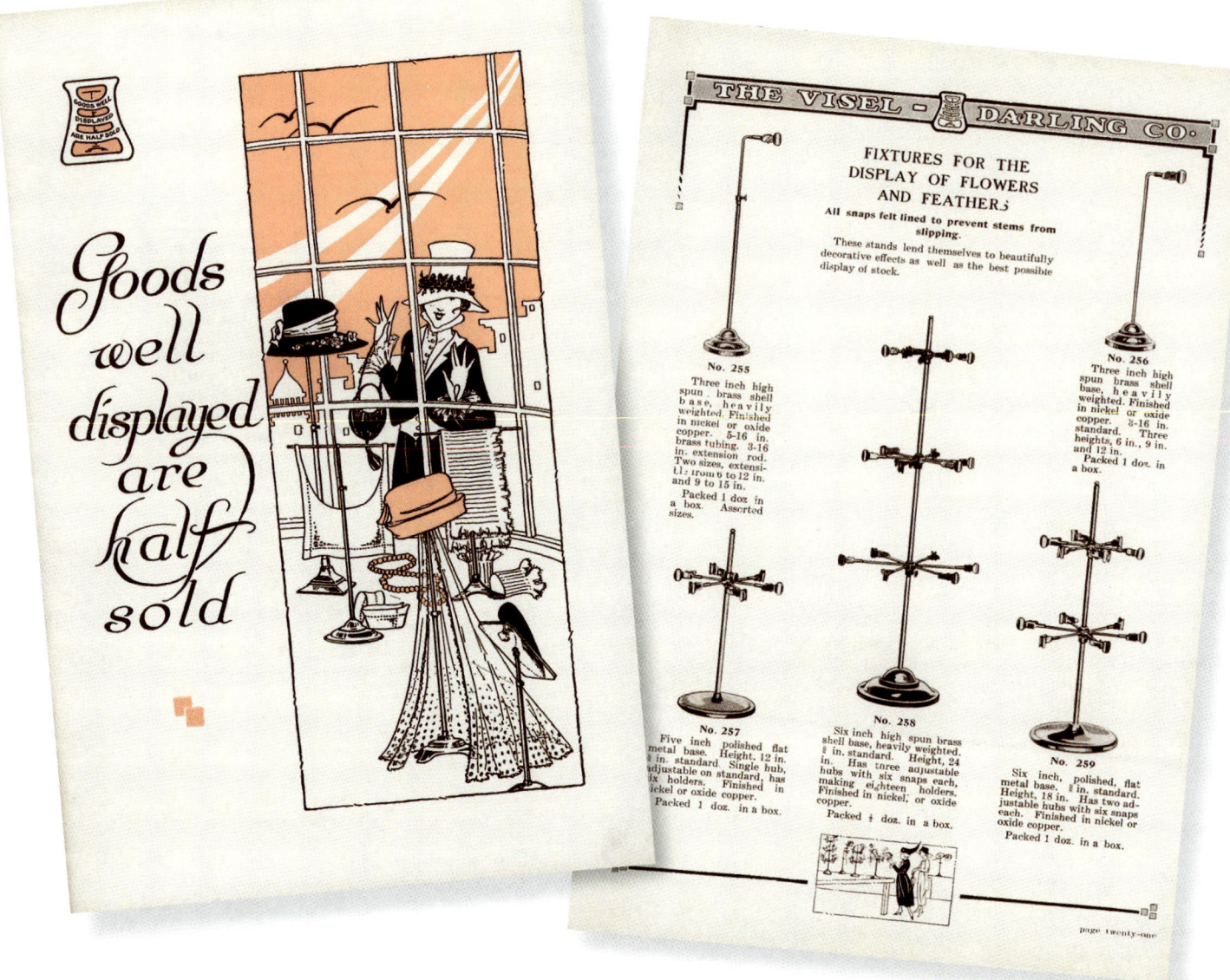

These illustrations appeared in an early Darling catalog.

*positions, and in no way will this affiliation alter operation of The Colson Corporation. Jay Pritzker, board chairman of Colson; Norman Price, executive vice president of Colson; and I are members of the Board of Directors of the L. A. Darling Company.*[11]

In 1959, the two companies had combined sales of $18.4 million ($7.4 million from Colson) and a net income of $1.03 million ($354,000 from Colson).[12]

**Reshaping Darling**

As with the other acquisitions, L. A. Darling needed some help. One of Bob's first moves was to spin off Midwest Foundry as its own company. The plant manager, Albert H. Doerr, was promoted to company vice president and general manager. At Doerr's suggestion, the foundry began to concentrate on producing small, high-volume shell castings. "That turned out to be a very successful strategy," said Bob. "For the next twenty years, it was a very profitable foundry with a 40 percent return on investment."[13]

The mannequin business of the Plastic Division was put under the control of George Jones, who spent ten years trying to "develop it into something."[14] Ultimately, however, the mannequin business would be divested.

In the fall of 1962, just as GAI had financed the move of Colson's caster production from Elyria to Jonesboro, L. A. Darling financed the move of Colson's truck manufacturing facilities from Elyria to Caruthersville, Missouri. With the help of cooperative local officials, Colson moved into a new, sixty-five-thousand-square-foot plant built at a cost of $186,000.

By this time, with new companies coming on board quickly, the Pritzkers realized they needed additional help, especially with the increasingly complex bookkeeping. In December 1960, Bob hired Charles Mertz, an accounting executive he had worked well with at the Rubatex division of Great American Industries. Mertz moved to Chicago to became treasurer of Colson and began to work with the controllers of all the operating units. In time, a system of dual-line reporting required all controllers to report to a corporate controller in Chicago, as well as to their own general managers.[15] This dual-reporting system, designed to keep Chicago informed of various operations, was to become a trademark of Marmon operations.

"Dual reporting meant that the local controller reports to their general manager for most things,

The Viz-U-Sell system was adjustable for a wide range of goods. These display products were manufactured in a plant in Bronson, Michigan. Although Viz-U-Sell was L. A. Darling's largest business at the time of the acquisition, the Pritzkers guessed that it would soon be outdated by newer display systems.

but for certain aspects, such as the quality of the bookkeeping, they report to both their general manager and corporate controller," Bob Pritzker said. "If there's a disagreement, my suggestion is to tell the general manager to call me or the corporate controller and say there's a problem. We will referee it."[16]

### Marmon-Herrington

In late 1962, the Pritzkers moved on another company, this time buying shares of the Indianapolis-based Marmon-Herrington Company. According to a January 1963 news report, L. A. Darling had acquired 206,000 of the 620,709 shares outstanding.

> *One hundred fifty thousand shares were purchased from Col. Arthur W. Herrington, a co-founder and chairman of M-H. . . . The additional 56,000 shares were acquired from other shareholders in an offer to purchase that expired Dec. 29. . . . At current bid prices, the Darling purchase would represent an investment of nearly $2,100,000.*[17]

The article, which appeared in the *Chicago Sun-Times*, also noted that Marmon-Herrington had posted a 1962 profit of $167,994 on sales of $17,757,138—not exactly a great profit margin.[18]

Marmon-Herrington had been founded in 1931 by Walter C. Marmon, former president of the defunct Marmon Motor Car Company, and Colonel Herrington. The Marmon Motor Car Company had gone bankrupt in 1930. The name and operation were preserved after Herrington bought the company's tooling with plans to begin production of four-wheel-drive vehicles. Marmon, however, was famous for another kind of car. It was a Marmon car—the Wasp—that won the first Indianapolis 500 Speedway race on May 30, 1911, averaging 74.61 mph.[19]

In 1931, Marmon-Herrington made its first four-wheel-drive vehicles. Herrington was a staunch advocate of four-wheel drive after seeing these vehicles cut through the French mud during a stint as an army truck driver during World War I.[20] By the time the United States entered World War II, Marmon-Herrington light combat tanks, four-wheel-drive vehicles, and half-track desert cruisers were in service with the British in North Africa and the Far East.[21]

After the war, Marmon-Herrington's 263,000-square-foot plant, a former Duesenberg automobile factory, began producing kits to turn conventional Ford trucks into all-wheel-drive vehicles. It also produced a line of electric trolleys, motor coaches, and other specialized commercial vehicles.

By the time Jay Pritzker met Arthur Herrington, Marmon-Herrington had expanded into a range of businesses that included Cardair, a small division that made specialized heavy-duty air compressors, and two joint-venture foreign affiliates: Cardox G.B., a manufacturer of nonexplosive blasting systems for use in gaseous mines, and Marmon-Bouquet, a builder of Marmon-Herrington all-wheel-drive vehicles for the French armed forces. The company's largest division was Long-Airdox, a West Virginia manufacturer of underground mining equipment.[22]

### Long-Airdox

Long-Airdox was a new addition to Marmon-Herrington. It had been acquired in 1960 from the Long family for a large block of Marmon-Herrington stock. For John B. Long, who handled the deal for

---

Opposite: Besides the store fixtures division, L. A. Darling had three other divisions. The Workwall Division, located inside Darling's main plant, at top, made mobile partitions for businesses. The Plastic Division, middle, made mannequins. And the Midwest Foundry, bottom, produced iron and steel alloy castings. The Pritzkers considered the foundry to be L. A. Darling's strongest business.

Right: The Marmon-Herrington logo. When it came time to name their growing enterprise, the Pritzkers turned to the Marmon identity because of its position of respect in the engineering community.

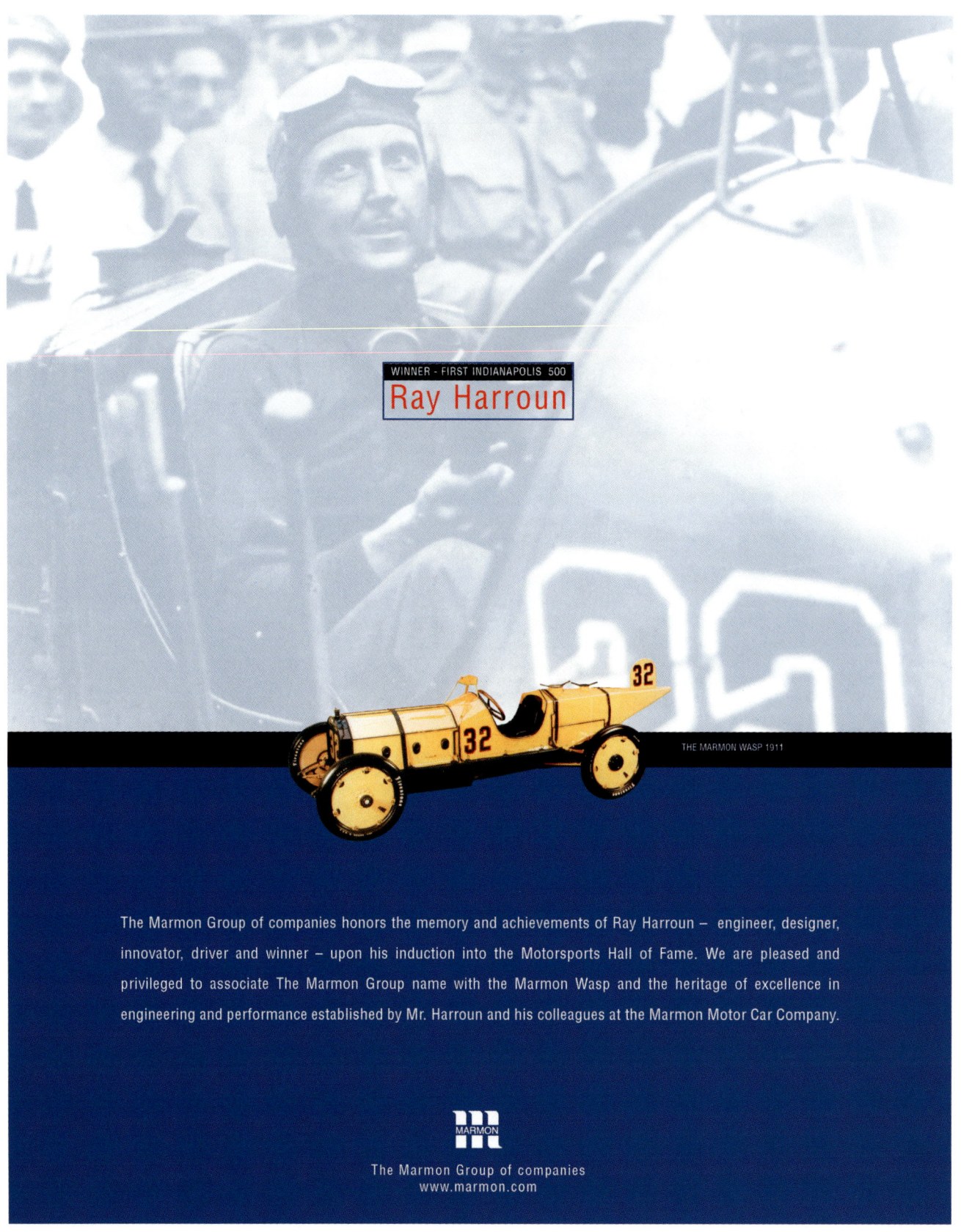

Opposite: The Marmon Wasp, created by the Marmon Motor Car Company and commemorated in this 2000 ad, won the first Indianapolis 500 race in 1911. The car averaged more than seventy-four miles per hour throughout the race.

his family the sale turned out to be a disappointing move because of Marmon-Herrington's precarious situation.

Marmon-Herrington had, by the end of the 1950s, already lost most of its defense business as well as its commercial transit trade. Worse yet, the aging board of directors, to which Long had been appointed, seemed to be living in the past and, as Jack Steinberg put it, "dreamt of corporate resurrection" despite year after year of losses. Unfortunately for Long, only Long-Airdox was profitable.

In a 1961 letter to Colonel Herrington marked "Personal and Confidential," Long wrote: "I am increasingly disturbed on each visit to Indianapolis. . . . I know of no logical basis for us to continue operations [there]. . . . Part of my reasoning is the doubt engendered by a five million dollar loss for the past five years of operations at Indianapolis."[23]

But Long was not to receive any relief until the Pritzkers bought the company. By 1963, Marmon-Herrington was effectively controlled by the Pritzkers and Long. In a board meeting that February, John Long was named president of Marmon-Herrington and immediately announced the election of a new seven-member board. All but Henry "Cap" Pascale, a wealthy investor who had been an American World War I flying ace and a member of the original board, were aligned with the Pritzkers.

Pascale, however, was trouble enough. He brought with him the previous directors' fears that the money-losing bus and truck operations and the once internationally renowned Indianapolis factory would be shut down. "The Colonel was wild about keeping the plant open," remembered Bob Pritzker. "At one board meeting, the subject came up of shutting the plant down, and the Colonel stood up in a rage."[24]

From the Pritzkers' point of view, there was ample justification for closing the factory: the plant was losing approximately fifty thousand dollars a month.[25] On June 25, 1963, John Long reported to the directors that the Indianapolis plant was to be swiftly shut down. After this announcement, developments unfolded rapidly.

On July 1, Marmon-Herrington purchased most of the assets of the Sanford Day Company for approximately seven hundred thousand dollars. The firm manufactured rail vehicles for underground mining at a seventy-five-thousand-square-foot plant in Knoxville, Tennessee. Besides strengthening Long-Airdox's already profitable product line, the purchase gave Marmon-Herrington a seventeen-acre site near Knoxville on which a new Long-Airdox plant could be built.

On July 2, Marmon-Herrington's heavy-duty truck business was sold to one of its Texas dealers. By mid-July, Marmon-Herrington's four-wheel-drive operations were moved into a small factory in Lebanon, Indiana, along with stockpiled replacement parts for Marmon-Herrington's commercial and military vehicles still in use throughout the world.

In late August, Marmon-Herrington's corporate headquarters were moved from Indianapolis to Oak Hill, West Virginia, the home of the Long-Airdox division, which had absorbed the Cardair division a month before.

In September, John Long's family sold its remaining Marmon-Herrington shares to L. A. Darling, boosting Darling's stake to 51.1 percent. The famed Indianapolis plant, which once produced tanks for the armies of Chiang Kai-shek, was finally put up for sale.[26]

On October 22, 1963, the Pritzkers incorporated a new holding company in Delaware, naming it after L. A. Darling's address in Bronson—the 606 Matteson Street Company.

This new corporation exchanged one thousand shares for all of the Darling stock owned by Pritzker trusts and all but nine shares of the James Foundry Corporation. (James Mfg. Co. remained a subsidiary of Rockwood & Company.) The new corporation then offered to buy all of Darling's assets, including its Colson and Marmon-Herrington stock, for $5.5 million and the assumption of all liabilities. After the transaction was approved by the stockholders on November 19, the Delaware firm was renamed Matteson Metals.[27]

Matteson Metals now controlled approximately 53 percent of Marmon-Herrington stock. It proposed to merge itself with Marmon-Herrington and create a larger corporate entity that would have sales of more than $28 million.

Under terms of the proposed merger, Marmon-Herrington shareholders would receive preferred stock in the new company valued at $11 a share in exchange for their common stock in Marmon-Herrington, which was then trading at $10 a share, even though it had a book value of $16.57.[28]

The merger was approved by shareholders on December 30, but the sole board member who voted against the move, Cap Pascale, sued in the local Indianapolis courts, claiming that the terms were unfair to minority shareholders. After the Pritzkers prevailed, Pascale sued again in federal court in Charleston, West Virginia, and had better luck. On March 21, 1964, the court issued a temporary injunction that stopped the merger.

That same month, Bob made a major change in his management team. He relieved Norman Price of his duties and replaced him with George Jones, who later moved from Arkansas to Chicago to become Marmon's vice president in addition to Colson's general manager. Jones was also given control over Long-Airdox, L. A. Darling, and the other companies. He ultimately became executive vice president of The Marmon Group.

While awaiting word on the Marmon–Matteson Metals merger, Bob turned his attention to the troubled James Mfg. Co. A long, steady drop in poultry and egg prices had forced James and its Atkinson Finance Company subsidiary to foreclose on many of their debtor customers. "For years," Bob remarked, "we owned and ran small poultry farms throughout the country."[29]

On July 23, the Pritzkers closed a deal to sell James Mfg. Co. to the Kansas City–based Butler Manufacturing Company, a large manufacturer of metal farm buildings. Not included in the sale, however, was James's plant in Fort Atkinson, which would be leased to Butler. The Pritzkers also retained the profitable James Foundry Corporation.

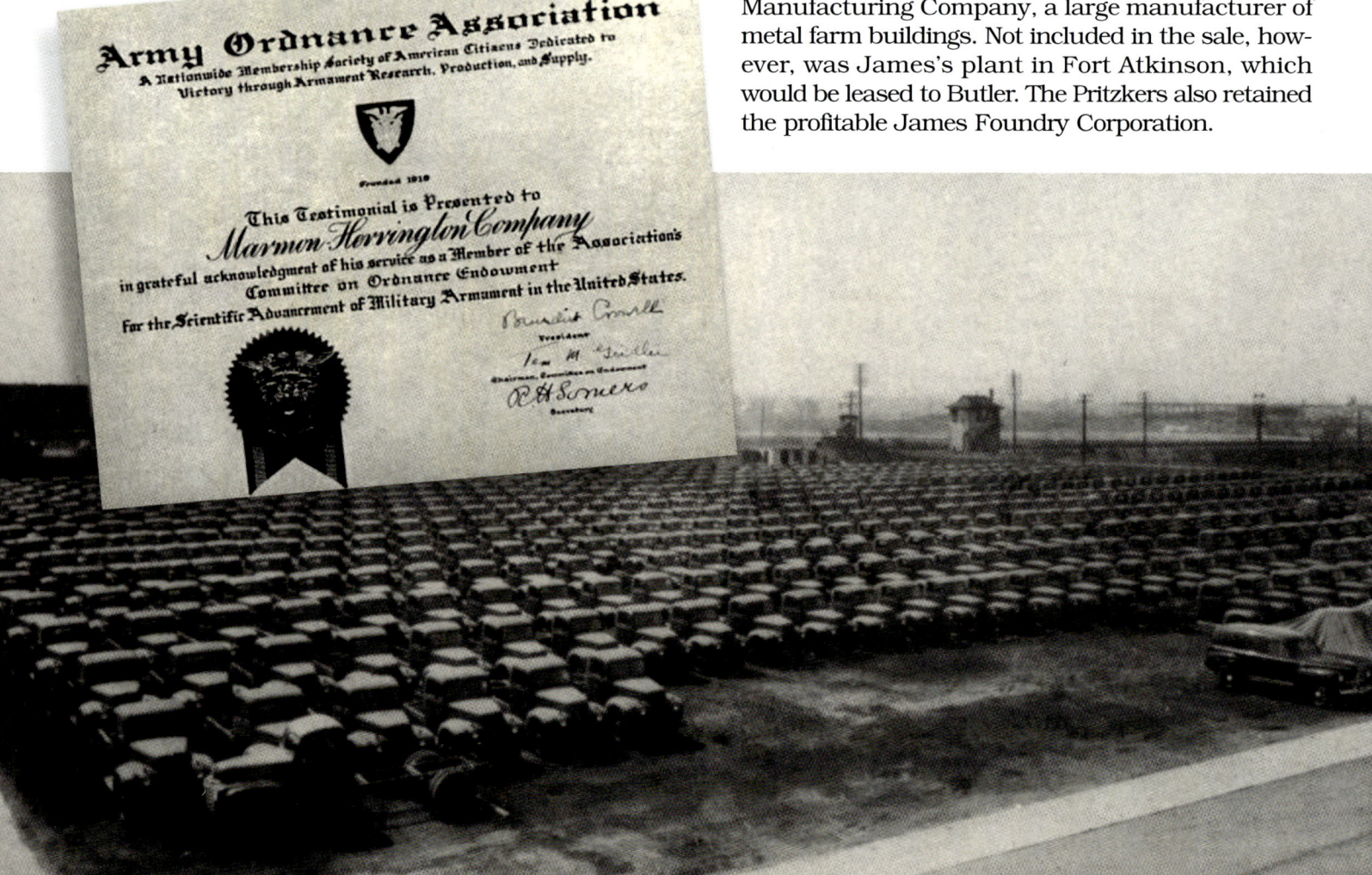

This page and opposite: Images from a Marmon-Herrington brochure printed in the 1950s. Under Col. Arthur Herrington, a veteran of World War I, Marmon-Herrington became one of the world's leading manufacturers and producers of four-wheel drive vehicles. By World War II, Marmon-Herrington vehicles were relied upon throughout the armed services for their dependability in all-terrain conditions. By the time the Pritzkers approached the company, however, much of its defense-related business had evaporated and Marmon-Herrington was financially unstable.

WALTER C. MARMON    A. W. HERRINGTON

# 10 Years before PEARL HARBOR—in Indianapolis, Indiana, Two Men "DECLARED WAR" Against the Enemies of Democracy

IT HAS BEEN SAID that America is the "Arsenal of the Democracies." If that is true, then The Marmon-Herrington Company can rightly be called the "Laboratory" of that arsenal—as the scores of military vehicle "firsts" which our company has created will confirm. Some, but not all of these vehicles, the "yesterdays of today's military vehicles," are shown in this book.

It was no literal declaration of war, of course, that Walter C. Marmon and Arthur W. Herrington, the founders of this company, made on March 13, 1931. Neither they, nor any other person knew then, just how and when the next war would start, or how the nations of the world would be aligned in the conflict.

But, even in 1931, the certainty of that conflict was apparent. Apparent too, were the part America would have to play, and her total unpreparedness for the part.

Let there be no misunderstanding. The welfare of our country was not alone the deciding factor that caused these men to found the company, and start originating, designing and building military vehicles. They also saw opportunity for profit, in adapting these new designs for unusually difficult civilian services.

As a Captain of the A.E.F. in France, during

Under terms of the sale, Butler was granted the rights to manufacture and market Jamesway products only in the United States. Bob kept Jamesway Company Limited, the unit set up to make and market Jamesway products in Canada. Under a separate deal, the European marketing firm Bob had established in Holland handled certain overseas areas of sales for Jamesway.

The parent company, Jamesway Co. Ltd., handled sales everywhere else. This agreement covered the right to market Jamesway's Big J, the innovative poultry feeding, watering, cleaning, and ventilation system, as well as other Jamesway products.

On another front, in May 1964 Bob completed the acquisition of Texas-based Amarillo Gear Works. The firm made gears that transmitted power from gas engines to deep-well water pumps used for agricultural irrigation in the western plains. The company, which occupied a forty-three-year-old, forty-thousand-square-foot plant near Amarillo, had sales that averaged $2.5 million a year. Soon after the acquisition, Bob began to seek new uses for the company's manufacturing capabilities.

"Amarillo Gear is a very profitable business, but extremely seasonal and cyclical," Bob said.

*The product is very expensive to make as well as the equipment to make it, so it would be most helpful if we could have a very similar product that was not so seasonal and counter-cyclical. Consequently, each time I visited Amarillo Gear, I would come up with a new idea of a market for our spiral bevel gears. Each time, the manager would patiently explain that my idea was a terrible one, and he was right. About the sixth time I tried, he stopped me before I could get through my first sentence. "Bob, I think I have the answer. We will make cooling tower gears whose cycle and season are not related to the agricultural gears." It turned out to be a great success and very much enhanced the profitability of the company as well as smoothing our employment. It was a wonderful solution for the company—the manager was proud of himself and he was pleased that I had stimulated the thought that solved the problem, even though I couldn't.*[30]

The new products, aimed at operating fans in water cooling towers, were a success.

### The Marmon Group

By this time, it was apparent that the organization needed a new name. The group of companies was steadily growing and branching into more and more markets. Moreover, the management approach had continued to evolve. The Pritzkers' various companies continued to be separately managed, regardless of any legal or corporate relationships. The general managers of each company were given great freedom to run their companies as they saw fit, and they carried the responsibility for making a profit. The system's true innovation was the bookkeeping relationship between the independent companies and the Chicago office. Each firm's general manager hired a controller, who reported to the manager as well as to a corporate controller based in Chicago.

While this system allowed for considerable leeway, having both general managers and controllers reporting to Chicago gave Bob Pritzker a considerable window into his operations. "The company controller was supposed to be very frank in his communications to whoever was the corporate controller at that time," George Jones said. "If he had differences of opinion with the general manager, he was expected to express them."[31]

When looking for a name for the organization, Bob wanted something that would allow for this unique management structure while acknowledging

The Marmon Group logo, introduced in the 1960s. As they expanded their organization, the Pritzkers wanted to maintain the companies' individual identities, brands, and leaders and designated them as "member companies" of the larger Marmon Group.

# CHAPTER TWO: THE MARMON GROUP IS BORN

Jay and Bob Pritzker, seated far left and far right, respectively, with some of the other family members and business associates. Youngest brother Don is seated next to Bob, while Uncle Jack Pritzker is standing in the back row on the far right. Bob and Jay's dad is sitting in the center, with his hands on his knees. The family had holdings in multiple industries and a successful law firm.

the enterprise's focus on manufacturing. Finally, he settled on The Marmon Group.

"The word 'Group' was rarely used in those days," Bob explained. "I chose it because I didn't want to create a monolithic entity. I wanted to make it clear that ours was a group of companies, not a corporation with a bunch of divisions."[32] Marmon, furthermore, had a historical association with engineering and manufacturing excellence.

Just two weeks after the sale of the James Mfg. Co., the U.S. District Court in Charleston, West Virginia, began to hear Cap Pascale's lawsuit to stop the Matteson Metals and Marmon-Herrington merger. After hearing from the attorneys on both sides, the judge insisted they reach a compromise. After negotiation, a price of $14.77 a share was agreed upon. It was less than the $16.57 per share book value but more than Jay's original offer of $11 a share. As for Pascale's concerns that the Indianapolis plant would be shut down, by the time the suit was heard, it had already been sold to a manufacturer of metal cookware, who ended up hiring many of the factory's former employees.

On November 18, 1964, Matteson Metals, Inc., was rechristened The Marmon Group, Inc. It was from this holding company that the modern Marmon Group borrowed its name. When The Marmon Group was created, its member companies numbered twelve—L. A. Darling, Midwest Foundry, James Foundry, Long-Airdox Company, Sanford Day, Cardox Great Britain, Marmon-Herrington Company, Amarillo Gear, Colson Corporation, Colson Canada Limited, Jamesway, and Associated Manufacturers International S.A.—and three affiliates: Marmon-Bouquet France, Prado Hermanos & Cia S.A. of Spain, and Industrias Metalicas Sudamericanas Limitada (IMSA) of Colombia, South America.

In 1964, these companies had combined sales of $47.04 million and earnings of $2.42 million.

The Keystone Pipe & Supply Company yard in the early 1930s. Keystone joined The Marmon Group in 1970.

CHAPTER THREE
# CONSOLIDATING GAINS
## 1965–1974

*Basically, we bought a dominant position in a public company, then proposed a merger for cash or securities, and finally we brought it private. That's the history of many of Marmon's deals.*

—Jay Pritzker, describing the
American Steel acquisition

BY THE MID-1960S, THE NEWLY denominated Marmon Group was solid. In 1965, the member companies' combined net revenues rose to $51.8 million, producing a net income of $3.1 million. This growth was accomplished even though no new acquisitions were made that year.[1]

In 1966, however, the acquisitions resumed. On July 6, 1966, Marmon-Herrington's Cardox Great Britain operation purchased Austin Hopkinson Limited of Manchester, England. Hopkinson manufactured heavy-duty winches and hoists for coal mines in England and Wales. The firm's business thrived from its founding in the early twentieth century through World War II, but then Britain's postwar Labor governments nationalized the coal-mining industry.

Bob gave the firm a new name, Pikrose & Company, and appointed a new managing director, on top of building a modern factory. Together these strategies attracted enough additional business abroad to maintain profitability for more than twenty years.

In the late 1980s, many of Great Britain's government-subsidized coal-mining operations were closed down by Margaret Thatcher's Tory government due to their inefficiency. That shrinking of the firm's customer base was sufficient to lead to the sale of Pikrose & Company and its assets in 1991.

### Fenestra

In 1966, the Pritzkers also agreed to buy Detroit-based Fenestra, a maker of flat-leaf springs for cars and trucks and of steel windows used in industrial construction. For most of its life since its founding in 1904 as the Detroit Steel Products Company,[2] the firm had been a success. In the late 1950s, though, due to a growing preference for aluminum windows in the construction trade and auto makers' switch from leaf to coil springs, business suffered greatly. By 1961, Fenestra had to drop its window line, which had accounted for the majority of its sales and profits.

The Pritzkers had invested five hundred thousand dollars in Fenestra stock, but their overtures to acquisition were rebuffed.[3] In 1963, a Florida-based land development company, the Gulf American Land Corporation, purchased approximately 37 percent of Fenestra stock.[4] As Jack Steinberg noted, Gulf American owner Leonard Rosen "apparently intended to liquidate Fenestra assets to support his land-development business."[5]

Fenestra's steel windows were popular up until the 1950s, when the advent of aluminum-frame windows weakened the company's market position. The company was forced to drop its line of windows in 1961.

Founded in 1904, the Detroit Steel Products Company later evolved into Fenestra, which the Pritzkers bought in 1966, after its trademark window line had been dropped.

Imagining that the Pritzkers and Gulf American were working together to dismantle Fenestra for their own gain, Fenestra's board of directors sued them. The case went all the way to the Michigan Supreme Court, but in April 1966, the court dismissed the charge of conspiracy as unfounded. Subsequently, Fenestra's board of directors and officers resigned and were replaced by others, including Jay.[6]

In November 1966, The Marmon Group, Inc., purchased Gulf American's stake in Fenestra for $21.50 a share and began to acquire more shares in the open market. Within a year, Marmon held a majority 69.3 percent stake in Fenestra.

On December 5, 1967, Fenestra swapped approximately two million shares of newly issued convertible preferred stock for complete ownership of The Marmon Group, Inc., and Jamesway. Fenestra's common stock was split two-for-one and its name changed to The Marmon Group, Inc. (Michigan). The Pritzkers now owned 84.3 percent of this new publicly held corporation. Colson was not included in the corporate restructuring and remained private.

### Mosaic Tile Company

"By then," Jay explained, "Marmon had become a good, growing business, generating good profits."[7] To help offset those rising profits, Jay set out to find a company with tax losses. He found the Mosaic Tile Company of Cleveland, Ohio.

Once one of the largest tile producers in the United States, publicly held Mosaic operated plants in New Jersey, Mississippi, and California. The Oxford Tile Company, a wholly owned subsidiary, operated two additional plants in Cambridge, Ohio. Due to management problems, as well as stiff foreign and domestic competition, Mosaic had recently suffered operating losses of $2 million. It was just the sort of scenario Jay was looking for.

On February 2, 1967, Marmon offered $14 a share for approximately half of the tile maker's 539,000 shares outstanding. At the time, Mosaic shares were trading on the Big Board for $7.75 to $8.50. The firm's president, however, urged shareholders to reject the deal, citing Mosaic's book value of approximately $32 a share and current asset value of approximately $19 a share.

In response, Marmon raised its offer to $15 a share, which proved sufficient to entice a majority of shareholders. On March 16, 1967, Marmon announced its ownership of 78 percent of the tile maker's shares. By June, it owned 98.3 percent, for which it had paid about $7 million.

In the spring of 1968, barely a year after Marmon purchased Mosaic, the Pritzkers received an offer to buy it. A growing competitor, the Boston-based Stylon Corporation, which was headed by a former tile setter named Joseph Mass, wanted to increase its market share by acquiring the long-established and more prestigious Mosaic Tile.

"Mosaic was losing money, but we had bought it for [less than half] of its book value," Bob explained. "On that sale we got essentially Mosaic's book value. When we deducted the money we'd lost operating it, we got double what we had paid for it."[8]

Mass didn't buy the Oxford Tile plants in Ohio or the Mosaic plant in Mississippi, however. "We kept them and ran them for seven years as Oxford Tile Company," Bob continued. "We made some money but eventually sold them and were out of the tile business."[9]

### Triangle Auto Spring

Although The Marmon Group was created through the purchase of financially compromised companies, as it grew, the Pritzkers were able to target more robust companies. One of these was the Triangle Auto Spring Company of DuBois,

Pennsylvania. Purchased by The Marmon Group, Inc. (Michigan), on December 31, 1968,[10] Triangle was a leading manufacturer of replacement flat-leaf springs for trucks and trailers and an important supplier of replacement springs for passenger cars.[11]

Bob went to see the firm's president, John C. Dunlap, after learning that Triangle—which had steady profits and sales of $3.4 million—was for sale. Dunlap's nonnegotiable asking price was exactly $3,006,000, even though the books were unaudited. After the meeting, Jay and Bob had a "rare board meeting" in the men's room to talk about it. There, they decided that Dunlap was totally trustworthy.

"It turned out that it was worth more than he said," Bob explained. "He was conservative about it. It was his nature to be conservative."[12]

The only cloud hovering over the deal was an antitrust suit threatened by a former Cleveland-based distributor. Triangle had bypassed the distributor by selling directly to automotive repair shops in his territory. Although the distributor had died, his son, who took over the business, was pressing on with the claim.

"Lawyers told me it would be a very expensive lawsuit for both sides," Bob explained. "I went to Cleveland to see the son. He said his father had been insulted and hurt, that he had done a good job, and that Dunlap had not been gracious about it. Also, there was a disputed charge for five thousand dollars and some inventory he was stuck with."[13]

In response, Bob offered to pay the disputed five thousand dollars and take back the inventory. The son accepted, with the stipulation that he also receive a letter of apology from Dunlap for the poor treatment his father suffered. While Bob ended up writing the letter himself, Dunlap was persuaded to sign it, and with Dunlap's signature the suit was dropped.

As noted in their first annual report to shareholders, Bob, as president, and Jay, as chairman of the board, were more than content with the first year of operations of their public company, The Marmon Group, Inc. (Michigan).

"We are pleased to report that earnings improved substantially during 1968. Operating profits before income taxes increased by 30 percent to $6 million and after-tax operating profits increased almost 20 percent to $3.3 million, while sales of continuing operations increased by 9 percent."[14]

When added to those of the private companies, the figures were even more impressive. In 1968, the total income of the Marmon companies was $87.4 million, up from $79.5 million the year before. After-tax profits increased to $3.8 million.[15]

In 1969, the numbers continued to climb. Sales for the combined public and private companies that year reached $94.1 million, with profits of more than $5 million.[16]

### The L. A. Darling Turnaround

Under Bob's organization, the businesses were clearly thriving, but the member companies trotted out a parade of challenges. By the mid-1960s, L. A. Darling's business was experiencing hard times.

An L. A. Darling display in the 1960s. By this time, the company's flagship product line, Viz-U-Sell, was coming under increasing competitive pressure from newer models.

In fact, during the Fenestra acquisition, Bob considered selling L. A. Darling.

The problem was fairly simple. J. C. Penney had stopped using the Viz-U-Sell shelving system, and the giant retailer had been L. A. Darling's best customer. Before long, other companies followed suit, opting for less costly display systems.

At a meeting to consider the company's fate, attended by Bob, Jay, and George Jones, Jones urged the Pritzkers to keep the company alive. "Jay thought we should close it, I was ambivalent, and George thought we should move it," Bob remembered. "We went with George because we felt he was closer to it and we had confidence in him."[17]

Based on Jones's recommendation, Darling moved from its inefficient plant in Michigan to a new, 83,000-square-foot factory in Paragould, Arkansas. The plant opened in 1966. Jones was made president, and Robert G. Harig, Darling's manufacturing vice president in Michigan, became the new general manager. By 1968, Darling had relocated its headquarters from Michigan to Paragould and expanded the Arkansas factory by 177,000 square feet. That April, Darling weathered another challenge. As the expansion neared completion, a nighttime tornado demolished the building that housed the steel bay area and tore the roof off much of the main production building, among other damage. Under Harig's leadership, production resumed the next day and Darling didn't miss a shipment to its customers. The following year, the plant was expanded by another 100,000 square feet, and Harig succeeded Jones as president, a position he would hold until his retirement in 1988.

Above and right: By the middle of the 1960s, L. A. Darling's traditional store display system had been dropped by J. C. Penney, and other major retailers were following suit. In response, Darling moved its production to Paragould, Arkansas, and changed its approach to service the new breed of giant merchandising chains like Wal-Mart.

# CHAPTER THREE: CONSOLIDATING GAINS

Darling's rapid expansion was fueled, in part, by the advice of a consultant who recommended that the company's business practices be restructured to serve the growing market of the large merchandising chains. Discount stores like Wal-Mart, which became a Darling customer, didn't need their stores planned for them, a service Darling had always provided in the past. What they needed was dependable delivery on short notice. With increased plant and warehousing capacity, Darling quickly developed a solid reputation as a quality, responsible supplier.

Improvements made in executive management, physical facilities, and manufacturing operations at other Group companies were also contributing to the increase in collective profits. Among the improvements to The Marmon Group's Chicago office team was the addition of attorney Walter R. Rogowski as general counsel. To oversee the recruitment of key executives of the member companies, particularly general managers and controllers, Bob hired L. William Emmert as the new vice president for personnel. Robert C. Gluth joined as corporate controller but quickly advanced to treasurer, then executive vice president overseeing all financial and tax matters.

This group, including George Jones and a few other executives who would join the company in the coming years, formed the core of the Chicago-based staff for many years to come.

**Keystone Pipe & Supply**

The last acquisition by The Marmon Group, Inc. (Michigan), as a public corporation was the 1970

The original Keystone Pipe & Supply building. The Pennsylvania company was founded in 1907 to distribute tubing. By 1970, when the company joined The Marmon Group, it had a national reach.

purchase of Keystone Pipe & Supply for $6,010,000. Founded in 1907, this Pennsylvania-based distributor of steel pipe and tubing had grown from a small, local supplier into a network of seven distribution centers located throughout the United States. It had sales in 1970 of $23 million and after-tax earnings of approximately $600,000.[18]

Renamed the Marmon/Keystone Corporation, during the next thirty years the firm expanded into a network of fifty sales and distribution centers in the United States, Canada, Mexico, and Europe.[19]

**Going Private:**
**American Steel & Pump**

In 1970, the Pritzkers completed the purchase of Fenestra and ended public ownership of The Marmon Group, Inc. (Michigan). A new holding company, the Bess Corporation, was incorporated in Delaware, and on December 15, 1970, The Marmon Group, Inc. (Michigan), was merged into

In early 1972, Marmon completed the acquisition of American Steel & Pump. Its flagship product was the Webb wheel, designed for trucks and trailers. As a member of The Marmon Group, Webb Wheel prospered.

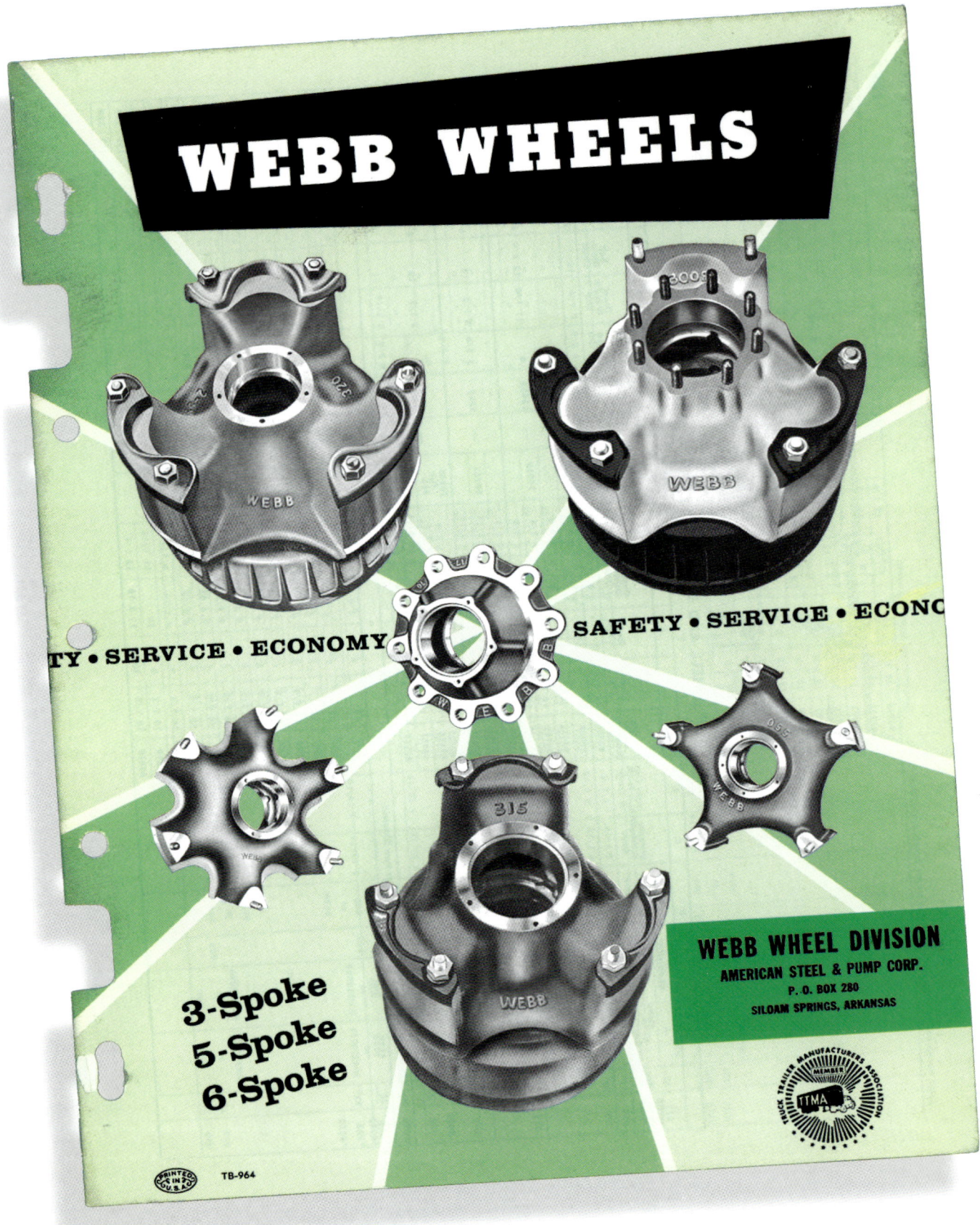

it. After Fenestra's preferred stock was converted to common stock, Bess then owned 91.1 percent. Under Delaware law, Bess had the authority to call in the 8.9 percent of shares it did not own. On November 11, 1971, remaining stockholders were notified that as "a first and final distribution," they would receive $12 per share. By the end of 1971, Fenestra was wholly owned, and the public company was gone.[20]

With The Marmon Group private once again, the Pritzkers set about to acquire the American Steel & Pump Corporation. The New York–based public firm was made up of seven smaller companies: a steel bar manufacturer, three steel bar distribution centers, two foundries that made steel castings, and a division called Webb Wheel, which made truck and trailer wheels. While American Steel's sales totaled $30.45 million, profits were small, debts large, and the plants old.

"Basically," Jay explained, "we bought a dominant position in a public company, then proposed a merger for cash or securities, and finally we brought it private. That's the history of many of Marmon's deals."[21]

This typically Marmon deal followed a familiar pattern: on March 11, 1971, a Pritzker-owned company purchased 74.5 percent of American Steel's shares for $8 a share, then tendered an offer to buy the rest. By December 16, the company had acquired more than 93 percent of all outstanding shares. Those shares were then transferred to a newly formed Delaware corporation which called in the rest of the stock in January 1972.

A 1964 Webb Wheel catalog sheet, opposite, and Webb Wheel logo, above. When Webb joined The Marmon Group, it was a distant third in its market. Through investment and additional acquisitions, Webb grew to be the industry leader in its market.

Part of the Pritzkers' total $6 million investment was soon recouped by selling off the steel bar manufacturer and two of the steel bar distributors. The remaining companies included Oklahoma Steel Castings, Webb Wheel Products, and Huron Steel. Oklahoma Steel was sold off in 1982 for $2.02 million. Detroit-based Huron Steel, the remaining steel bar distributor, proved to be a steady moneymaker. The biggest prize, however, turned out to be Webb Wheel Products. Ranked a distant third in its industry when acquired by the Pritzkers, Webb introduced new products made in new, improved facilities and saw its sales soar from $7.8 million in 1971 to about $175 million in 2000, making it the undisputed leader in its industry.[22]

**Marmon Transmotive**

In 1969, John Long resolved to move Sanford Day mining products and Long-Airdox into a newly constructed plant in Knoxville, Tennessee. The plant was built at the request of Long, who had been enormously helpful and wanted to move to Knoxville. The plant was originally designed to manufacture both Sanford Day mining rail vehicles and Long-Airdox coal conveyor systems, but Long-Airdox executives refused to move the company from its established home in Oak Hill, West Virginia. Instead, some "odds and ends" were moved in with Sanford, including Marmon-Herrington's four-wheel-drive truck conversion kits and the manufacture of a hybrid road/rail maintenance vehicle called the Universal Track Machine. In 1974, the Knoxville operation was named Marmon Transmotive.[23] It was sold after Long retired.

At the end of 1974, The Marmon Group was flourishing. Combined sales reached $332.6 million, with annual earnings of $19 million.[24]

Molten metal at a Cerro Copper Products operation. The acquisition of Cerro Corporation in 1976 was the largest yet.

CHAPTER FOUR

# THE END OF THE BEGINNING
## 1975–1981

*My wife woke me up and said, "You need to go directly to Jay's office. Don't go to your office. You're going to borrow $700 million today for this acquisition."*

—Bob Gluth, remembering the 1981 Trans Union acquisition

AMONG THE MANY DEALS ENGIneered by the Pritzkers, the merger with Cerro Corporation was one of the largest. The deal added a new group of companies that had sales and assets nearly twice as large as The Marmon Group. Cerro sales in 1973 totaled $636 million. With businesses in both North and South America, as well as other parts of the world, Cerro Corporation was ranked high on the *Fortune* 500 list of major industrial firms.[1]

Founded in 1902, Cerro was one of the largest mining concerns in the world. It began after an American prospector rediscovered a long-abandoned 270-year-old Spanish silver mine at a place called Cerro de Pasco, at an elevation of some fifteen thousand feet in the central Andes of Peru. What he found was a rich deposit of copper ore laced with silver and gold, as well as one of the richest deposits of lead-zinc ore ever discovered.

Eventually, Cerro's collection of mines, smelters, and refining facilities grew to employ fifteen thousand workers. By 1974, the publicly owned American corporation had become Peru's largest business, employer, and taxpayer.

Cerro's size and foreign ownership made it a target for the Peruvian military government's program of nationalization, begun in 1968, when Gen. Juan Velasco Alvarado overthrew elected President Fernando Belaunde Terry. At the time of the coup, three-quarters of mining, one-half of manufacturing, two-thirds of the commercial banking system, and one-third of the nation's fishing industry were under direct foreign control.[2] By 1974, Peru's expropriation and nationalization of Cerro's mining, smelting, and refining operations were complete. A similar expropriation program by the socialist government in neighboring Chile had already stripped Cerro of its 70 percent stake in a major copper mining and refining facility in Rio Blanco.

Even with the loss of its Peruvian and Chilean components, Cerro remained a formidable business enterprise because of its aggressive expansion program in the 1950s. In the United States, Cerro acquired a large New York City–based fabricator of building wire and utility cable, Cerro Wire & Cable Company. In East St. Louis, Illinois, Cerro Copper Products smelted copper scrap, refined electrolytic copper, and made copper tubing for plumbing, refrigeration, and air-conditioning applications. In Bellefonte, Pennsylvania, Cerro Metal Products was a large producer of brass mill products, die castings,

---

The Trans Union logo, taken from a 1979 annual report. In 1981, Trans Union, an offspring of the Standard Oil Trust, joined The Marmon Group. Trans Union replaced Cerro as the largest acquisition in Marmon's history.

Cerro Corporation had various operations at the time of the acquisition. Scrap copper (left) sits in front of the Shelbina, Missouri, plant. Below, a billet casting furnace melts copper and turns it into usable billets. The cylinders (bottom) are examples of Cerro's copper tubing. At one time, Cerro had been the largest industry in Peru, but just before the Marmon acquisition, a new government nationalized the Andes mines.

and machined parts. Cerro also owned a Connecticut-based manufacturer of insulated wire called the Rockbestos Company. In 1973, the combined sales of these firms exceeded $500 million.[3]

Under the direction of its then president, C. Gordon Murphy, Cerro was a company in trouble when Jay Pritzker discovered it. By late 1973, a string of questionable investments—including Murphy's purchase of a stereo-tape club that ended up being sold at a loss of $4.5 million—had weakened the firm. At the same time, after negotiations with the United States, the governments of Chile and Peru had agreed to pay compensation for nationalizing Cerro and other American firms. From Chile, Cerro received $3.2 million in cash, plus $38.6 million in government notes.[4] From Peru, the corporation received $48 million in cash and the promise of $10 million more from a fund established to compensate U.S. companies.[5] In addition, due to the losses suffered in Peru, Cerro could claim a $135 million tax loss that could be used to offset taxes during the next ten years.[6] With another $70 million in cash on its balance sheet, Cerro was a perfect target for bear-market bargain hunters.

Hoping to diminish the possibility of a hostile takeover, Murphy sought the protection of the Pritzkers, with whom he had done business in the past. In early 1974, the Pritzkers' GL Corporation—one of the family's holding companies—acquired 813,000 shares of Cerro for between $17 and $18.50 a share, representing about 14 percent of all shares outstanding. Jay then joined the firm's board of

# CHAPTER FOUR: THE END OF THE BEGINNING

Below are copper billets, the raw material Cerro drew into copper tubing. At right, an employee winds finished tubing before shipment. Typical of Marmon, after the acquisition the Pritzkers sold off portions of the business that didn't fit with its core competencies.

directors, and Bob came on shortly afterward. They soon put together a coalition to eventually oust Murphy because, as Jay put it, "We found ourselves disagreeing with most of Murphy's business judgments."[7]

In June 1974, the Pritzkers' holding company made a tender for an additional 1.5 million shares at $19 a share. That would be enough to establish working control of Cerro. The Pritzkers were surprised, however, when they received tenders of 3.2 million shares from the stockholders.

"We had no idea so much stock would be tendered. We were inundated," Jay said.

> *Cerro had a tax-loss carryforward of $135 million. A section of the tax code stipulated that if 50 percent of the stock were to be acquired by five stockholders or less, we could lose the tax-loss carry forward. We had to decide how many shares we could safely purchase. We could even lose the tax loss if another, unrelated buyer accumulated enough to put us over the 50 percent threshold. We decided to take the risk that nobody else would buy that quantity, and we ended up acquiring up to the 45 percent level.*[8]

In September 1974, Cerro and GL announced they had agreed in principle to merge Cerro with The Marmon Group, Inc. Then on September 20, plans for the merger were abruptly suspended until late in 1975.[9]

As Jay explained it, "Our lawyers had made an error. There is a section of the Securities Code,

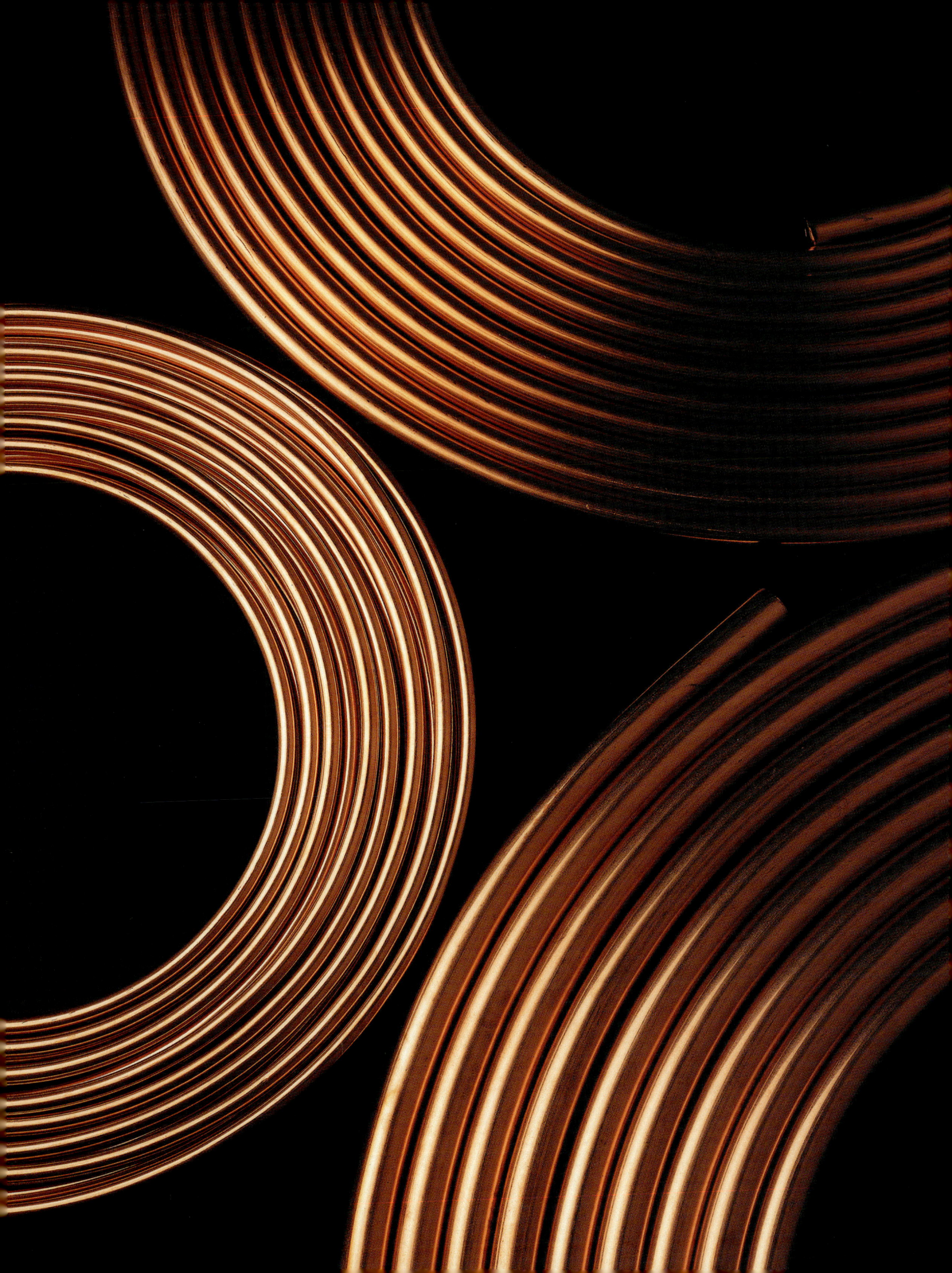

# CHAPTER FOUR: THE END OF THE BEGINNING

Right: This map appeared in a Cerro annual report in 1960, before the Peruvian and Chilean governments nationalized its operations. The map shows Cerro's extensive holdings in North and South America.

Opposite: The copper tubing business was retained after the acquisition and became a solidly profitable operation.

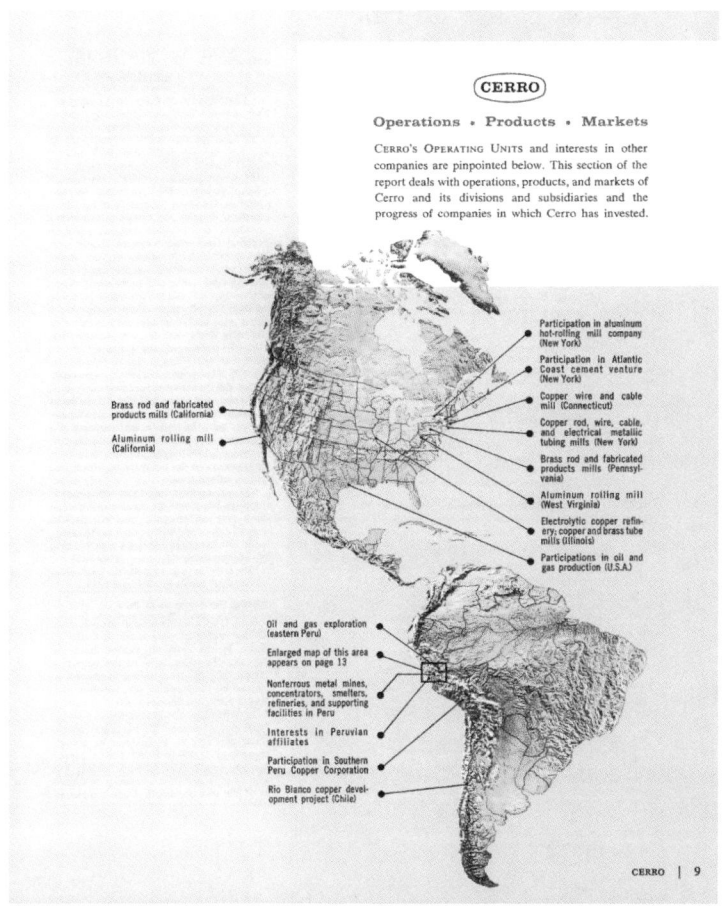

16-B, that prohibits short-swing profits—profits by an insider that occur within a period of six months. We were clearly insiders, and the fact that we had bought this stock and then were going to do a merger could be construed under 16-B to be a purchase and a sale. There would be no profit, but it's a technicality that could have created serious problems. To avoid them, we postponed the merger until the six-month period was past."[10]

During this waiting period, Murphy agreed to resign—for a price. In exchange for his resignation, he received $1.95 million in cash, plus office space and a secretary for six months at a cost to Cerro of $16,000.[11] Bob succeeded him as president; Jay, replacing Charles B. Harding, became chairman of the board.

Even though Cerro's 1974 sales rose 19 percent to $738.3 million, the firm was still in trouble. Most of the gain accrued from its metal-manufacturing companies, from its acquisition of a group of small western Pennsylvania coal companies, and from the purchase of a controlling interest in the Golconda Corporation, a producer of copper and brass fittings and controls for pressurized gases.[12] The corporation's real estate group, however, was losing money quickly due to a shrinking U.S. economy and soaring interest rates.

On April 9, 1975, the *Wall Street Journal* reported, "According to recent filings with the Securities and Exchange Commission, Cerro's Leadership Housing subsidiary is in dire financial straits and could go out of business at any time. The loss of the entire investment could cost Cerro $65 million."[13]

With Murphy gone and the merger plans on hold, Bob began to cut costs. Cerro's corporate headquarters were moved from New York to Marmon's small office in Chicago. Its staff was trimmed to six. "Bob did a very good job of closing down the home office almost immediately and selling off some of the assets that we just didn't want anything to do with," remarked longtime Marmon executive George Jones.[14]

In November 1975, the merger was back on. According to the *Wall Street Journal*, "Cerro Corp. said it will ask its shareholders to vote—probably in January—on a proposal to combine Cerro with Marmon Group Inc. and to exchange publicly held Cerro shares for preferred stock in the new company to be known as Cerro-Marmon Corp."[15]

Under terms of the proposed deal, Cerro's common stock would be exchanged one-for-one for preferred stock in the new company and would be redeemable for $22 a share. It would pay an annual dividend of $2.25 a share and would be noncallable for five years. A sinking fund commencing in the sixth year would retire 6.66 percent of the preferred shares each year, retiring the entire issue by the twentieth year after issuance.[16]

News of the proposed merger didn't sit well with some long-term Cerro investors, specifically with Josef Kaszovitz and Sully Schulwolf, who sought a preliminary injunction to stop the planned February 24 shareholder vote in New York.

"The shareholder suit said that the preferred shares received in exchange for Cerro common would preclude participation in any possible growth in Cerro's future earnings or financial well being," reported the *Wall Street Journal*. "As a result, the suit continued, one effect of the merger would be to 'freeze out' Cerro public shareholders from this 'residual equity.'"[17]

The state court judge who heard their request didn't agree, and the vote went ahead as scheduled. When the final tally was in, 82.1 percent of the shareholders approved of the merger. And although Jay got his way, he "conducted the meeting amid frequent harsh criticism of his family's motives for the merger," the *New York Times* reported.[18]

During a news conference held after the meeting, Jay "described the old Cerro as a 'troubled company with spotty earnings' and insisted that the stockholders who opposed what his management was doing 'suffered their losses years ago because of an unfortunate series of events that forced their stock down,'"[19] referring to the expropriation of Cerro's mines and the company's investment in the troubled Leadership Housing division.

Once the merger was complete, the Cerro-Marmon Corporation's 1976 sales of $905 million placed it at number 249 on the *Fortune* 500 list of the largest U.S. companies.[20]

After Cerro had been absorbed, Bob began to improve the company's earnings by selling off the problems he couldn't fix and reinvesting in areas likely to produce the greatest returns. For example, the Illinois-California Express trucking companies were sold, as well as mines and ore-processing plants in Greece, Tasmania, Kentucky, and Peru.

Similarly, Bob acted to improve the potentially profitable parts of the company. For example, he promoted Harold Lewin to general manager of Cerro Copper Products. Lewin had been the copper buyer but "kind of treated as a poor relation by the people who ran the company," remembered George Jones. "But he knew all about it. He knew what should have been done as well as what was being done, and he did very well."[21]

**Penn Aluminum**

In order to avoid confusion over the names of the various Pritzker-owned or -controlled businesses, in January 1977 the name of the public Cerro-Marmon Corporation was changed to The Marmon Group, Inc. The Cerro-Marmon name was used only by its coal mining companies thereafter. All other private firms were simply called members of The Marmon Group and retained their original names.[22]

Throughout the 1970s, the acquisitions continued unabated. In June 1971, five years before the merger with the Cerro Corporation, a broker approached Bob and asked if he'd be interested in buying a company called Penn Brass & Copper. The business was a struggling forty-eight-year-old company with a 128,000-square-foot factory. At first, Bob declined.

"I said that we weren't interested unless they wanted to give it away," Bob remembered. "Then I saw a photo showing that the plant was contiguous to one of our existing plants."[23]

By a strange turn of luck, Penn Brass & Copper happened to be located next to Fenestra, a growing company that was in need of additional warehouse space. Bob resolved to buy the company, "if only for the land."[24]

After the acquisition, Bob turned to Joel F. Lehman, Fenestra's controller, to run Penn Brass & Copper. "I told him: 'Run it as long as you can, reduce inventory each month, don't hire anyone, don't fire anyone, help people get other jobs, and don't lose money,'" Bob recalled.[25]

However, by dropping money-losing product lines, cutting costs, and increasing the productivity of his employees, Lehman had turned the company around by the end of 1972.

"The first month, they made twelve dollars," Bob remembered. "The next month, they made twenty-five thousand dollars. The third month, they made one hundred thousand dollars, and he said, 'I want to talk to you about this.' I told him that I was getting on a plane to see him. We bought the company for the land, which turned out to be worthless, but the company was valuable."[26]

Then, during one of several sales calls in Europe to drum up new business, Lehman was asked by Volkswagen if his small firm could produce aluminum tubing for use in the automaker's newly designed lightweight car radiators. After much retooling and six months of trial and error, Lehman was able to meet the demanding specifications of Volkswagen, and Penn received its first order. Other orders followed from radiator manufacturers in France and Italy. Indeed, the use of aluminum tubing was on the increase by European and American car makers and in other industries.

With the future looking bright for aluminum products, the company changed its name from the Penn Brass & Copper Company to Penn Aluminum International in August 1977. The firm's copper product lines, which had accounted for 80 percent of Penn's total business, were turned over to the larger, more efficient Cerro Copper Products plant in nearby Cleveland, Ohio.

In an effort to develop a Canadian counterpart to the highly successful Triangle Auto Spring Company, the Pritzkers turned to Montreal in January 1977. There they acquired two companies: the McRobert Spring Company, a producer of flat-leaf springs for trailers and trucks, and Inter-City Auto Parts, an automotive suspension parts distributor. Later on, an additional Montreal-based spring maker, Automotive Springs, was acquired. Eventually, McRobert closed its outdated plant and moved into a new production facility in Cambridge, Ontario.

**Breaking the Billion-Dollar Barrier**

With the addition of its new auto spring manufacturing and distribution business in Canada, sales of The Marmon Group at the end of 1977, the first full year after the Cerro Corporation merger, passed the billion-dollar mark: $1.3 billion. Earnings that year rose to $50.6 million.[27]

Marmon's last major acquisition during the 1970s was the California-based American Safety Equipment Corporation. Founded in the early 1950s as a marketer of men's and boys' leather belts, it grew into a public company that manufactured seat belt systems for autos and aircraft. Through its purchase of a British licensee, Kangol Magnet, it expanded into the overseas seat-belt market while continuing to manufacture Kangol's famous line of men's and women's hats, along with other apparel and safety-related goods. At the time American Safety joined The Marmon Group, the firm had twenty-three manufacturing and distribution centers in the United States,

Canada, and England, and employed thirty-five hundred. It earned $3.1 million on total sales of $95.4 million.

American, however, had its share of troubles. Though auto seat belts accounted for 63 percent of its sales, it did not have major supplier contracts with any of the large automakers. Also, the auto seat-belt market faced uncertainty because of unpredictable federal government safety

American Safety Equipment, acquired in the late 1970s, manufactured a variety of products, including seat belts like this one. As a member of The Marmon Group, Am-Safe, Inc., would become the largest manufacturer of airplane seat belts in the world.

requirements and the threat of air bags becoming standard equipment.

Nonetheless, Bob and Jay saw value in the firm, and in July 1978, a merger with a subsidiary of The Marmon Group, Inc., was approved at a cost of $27.3 million. Upon taking control, Bob sold off five of American's least promising subsidiaries, which had the effect of reducing the total investment in American Safety to approximately $23 million.

By the end of 1979, driven forward by strong performance in many of its member companies, Marmon's total sales neared $2 billion, while earnings increased to $79.2 million.[28]

**The Trans Union Deal**

At the beginning of the 1980s, The Marmon Group was about to embark on another massive and transformative acquisition. This time, efforts would focus on the purchase of the Trans Union Corporation, a giant, multifaceted company with roots all the way back to the early days of Standard Oil.

The thrust to purchase Trans Union began in late 1980 when Jerome Van Gorkom, chairman and CEO of Trans Union, called Jay and requested a meeting. At the meeting, Van Gorkom caught Jay completely off guard, proposing a merger between Trans Union and The Marmon Group.

As Van Gorkom explained years later during an interview, "I wasn't even sure that a company like Trans Union would even be interesting to private buyers, so I decided to talk to Jay on the general idea of the company's appeal to a buyer such as the Pritzkers."[29]

At the time, Trans Union was considered to be among the oldest and most respected of public companies. It was founded in the early 1870s by John D. Rockefeller as the Union Tank Line to move petroleum from Pennsylvania oil fields to his Standard Oil refineries in Cleveland and Chicago. Rockefeller's total control over the tankers used to transport oil made it an important part of his multicompany production and marketing monopoly known as the Standard Oil Trust.

As a result of the U.S. Supreme Court's 1911 landmark decision to bust the Standard Oil Trust, the Union Tank Line was spun off as a separate, independent lessor of rail tank cars. Its corporate name was officially changed to the Union Tank Car Company in 1919.[30] At the time of Jay's meeting with Van Gorkom, it owned sixty-three thousand tank and bulk cargo shippers, giving it the second largest tank-car fleet in the world.

Though the leasing of railcars was by far Trans Union's largest business, throughout the years it had diversified into a variety of other industries as well—from the development and sales of condominiums in California and Illinois, to the manufacture of water treatment equipment, to consumer credit reporting services.

Trans Union, as Van Gorkom explained to Jay, was solid. Its assets were valued at $1.7 billion, and in 1979 it had earned $60.7 million on revenues of $922.5 million. But Wall Street's interest in the public company's stock was disappointingly low. Despite a 90 percent increase in paid dividends, its average stock price in 1979 had appreciated only approximately 7 percent since 1970.[31]

Left: The Densmore car of 1865, one of the first "tank cars" in existence. This crudely constructed hauling vehicle consisted of two wooden vats mounted on a flatcar. In later generations, it gave way to the more recognizable tubular tank car, which was used by Standard Oil to haul crude.

Opposite, bottom: This more familiar tank car, one of the oldest Union Tank cars ever photographed, predates 1919, when the Union Tank Line officially changed its name to the Union Tank Car Company.

# CHAPTER FOUR: THE END OF THE BEGINNING

From left, George Jones, Bob and Jay Pritzker, and Bob Gluth. This group of executives negotiated the acquisition of Trans Union, which joined The Marmon Group in early 1981. It was the largest company ever to join The Marmon Group.

Trans Union's greatest appeal was in its tax credits amassed against the depreciation of its rail cars. In 1980, Congress was contemplating an even larger increase in the railcar depreciation rate, and Trans Union already had more depreciation available for tax purposes than it could use. Additionally, that depreciation eliminated Trans Union's income tax liability and prevented it from using the investment tax credit because that credit could be used only to offset income tax liabilities; all of which, Van Gorkom reasoned, made Trans Union vulnerable to a less-than-friendly takeover by a company in need of tax relief.[32]

Van Gorkom reasoned that Trans Union would probably be worth more to private owners than to a public company because a private owner would value the firm on the basis of cash flow rather than share earnings. Trans Union's cash flow per share at that time was almost three times its earnings per share.[33]

According to Jack Steinberg, Marmon's resident historian, a few days after Jay's meeting with Van Gorkom, Jay, Bob, and a small staff began to analyze the limited information they had on Trans Union.

Bob Gluth, a Marmon vice president, had just returned from his honeymoon when the merger discussion began. "My wife woke me up and said, 'You need to go directly to Jay's office. Don't go to your office. You're going to borrow $700 million today for this acquisition,'" Gluth remembered.[34]

As the group put the financing in place, Jay assembled the bare bones of a deal. He proposed a cash merger at $55 a share to be completed in January 1981 and the right to buy one million shares at $38 a share.[35] He also wanted the right to purchase the stock as compensation if Marmon lost to a higher bid, and he offered Trans Union the freedom to solicit alternative bids during the 60 to 120 days it would take to arrange the deal and get shareholder approval.[36]

Trans Union counted among its businesses a retail credit information reporting company. This division would grow into the largest consumer credit reporting agency in North America.

The deal was quick, but that's how Van Gorkom wanted it, remembered Bob Pritzker.

*He had three choices. He was piling up tax credits faster than he could use them. He could buy a company that needed them. He could sell it to a company. Or he could auction it. He didn't want an auction, and he didn't have the funds to buy a company. So he decided to see how much money he could get for it.*

*He came to $55 a share and he wanted to move fast. He needed somebody who had money and interest. There was also some internal tension with some of the managers, who wanted to do a leveraged buyout.* [37]

Van Gorkom arranged for a board meeting that evening. Before the meeting, he assembled his top executives and shared with them for the first time the details of Jay's offer. It wasn't very well received, largely because of some managers' desires to buy Trans Union themselves. Trans Union's chief financial officer and executive vice president, Donald B. Romans, insisted that a better price could be obtained and said he was looking at the possibility of a leveraged management buyout.

But as the *Chicago Tribune* noted, "Van Gorkom was against a leveraged buyout because he believed there were conflicts of interest in management becoming potential buyers." [38]

During the board meeting, Van Gorkom explained the proposed deal, along with his insistence that it be approved by Monday or else rejected. The directors voted to accept the deal, which assured shareholders of $55 a share if they wanted it. The directors also knew that under terms of Jay's proposal, they had the right to consider higher offers.

"That night," wrote Steinberg, "[Jay] and Van Gorkom signed the completed documents, and the following day—Saturday, September 20—news of the merger was released to the press." [39]

Still, however, the news did not sit well with Trans Union management. A group of executives led by Donald Romans decided to attempt a leveraged buyout. The situation was further complicated by the letters of resignation pouring in to the board from key executives stating they'd quit if the merger went through. Especially troubling was the letter from Jack Kruizenga, president of Trans Union's most significant subsidiary, the Union Tank Car Company.

"Nineteen letters were written to the board," Bob remembered. "The people who wrote them were crucial. . . . How were we going to run this company if no one's there?" [40]

As a result of the uproar, Van Gorkom called Jay and asked if he would withdraw the merger offer. Jay, knowing a good deal when he saw one, refused. He said, however, that he would give Trans Union until January 31, which was more than four months away, to attract a better offer.

Above: The manufacturing operation at a Union Tank Car Company plant.

Right: During production, huge cylinders are welded end to end, then capped at both ends. Union Tank is the largest lessor of railroad tank cars in the country.

Trans Union immediately set out to find a better deal. The company secured the services of Salomon Brothers, and the large investment banking firm compiled a list of more than one hundred possible suitors. Also, the executives interested in a leveraged buyout had sufficient time to put one together. But rising interest rates and a power struggle with the billionaire Reichmann family of Toronto, Canada, who were in on the deal, caused it to fall apart.

Likewise, a potential deal with General Electric arranged by the Salomon Brothers came undone for several reasons, including the merger's possible effect on the value of GE's stock, as well as Jay's refusal to agree not to top the $60-per-share offer if GE decided to make it. "We lucked out," remembered Bob, "because Jack Welch had just been named CEO, and he didn't want his first act to be buying a company."[41]

Since no one had come up with an offer better than the Pritzkers', when Trans Union's board met on January 26, 1981, the merger was approved. The following month, 70 percent of the votes of Trans Union shareholders were cast in favor of the deal as well.

"When the stockholders voted on February 10, 1981, to accept the Pritzker offer, they knew that Salomon Brothers had been beating the bushes for four months and could never get a better offer," Van Gorkom explained.[42]

The price the Pritzkers paid to conclude the Trans Union merger was $688 million.[43]

As usual, the task of getting the new acquisition to work was largely Bob's. "Trans Union was a hodgepodge," he said, "but we were used to hodgepodges."[44] While most of Trans Union's business operations were retained, there were notable divestitures. For example, the finance leasing company was eventually divested.[45] Other businesses divested by the early 1990s included a provider of computerized systems for credit unions, a Canadian lease-finance firm, and a large U.S.-Canadian renter of data communications and electronic test equipment.

Some of the other companies would evolve into major success stories. One of these was the credit information reporting firm, named Trans Union Credit Information. At the time of the merger, the company had a computer database covering consumers in twenty-three states. After Bob approved the investment of tens of millions of dollars, it became the largest consumer credit reporting agency in the entire country and expanded its coverage into Canada, Mexico, Europe, Africa, and Asia.

"That success was mainly because Bob Pritzker had a lot of faith and approved the money to improve it," Gluth commented.[46]

For the most part, however, management of Trans Union and its various remaining companies was left up to executives in the company. Gerald Shannon, an executive vice president with Trans Union before the acquisition, remained with the company in a leadership role and reported directly to Bob Pritzker after Trans Union had been taken private. Sidney Bonser, another Trans Union executive, became president of Union Tank Car Company. Both men became senior vice presidents of The Marmon Group.

"One of the advantages of working with The Marmon Group is you sit down and talk to the president and make a decision," Shannon said. "You don't write a big book like you have to do in a public company and then hopefully get on the docket and make a presentation to the board to get approval to do something. With Marmon, we could just sit down and have a discussion and move ahead."[47]

This sense of freedom from bureaucracy was discovered by many of the Trans Union executives who made the jump from a large public company to a privately owned concern.

**The Shareholders' Suit**

A short time after the Trans Union merger, a class action suit was initiated in Delaware by two shareholders. The suit sought either to rescind the merger or to receive damages from the former Trans Union board members equal to the difference between the $55 per share merger price and the "fair value" of the stock as determined by the court. While Jay and The Marmon Group were initially named as codefendants, the Delaware Chancery Court dismissed them as defendants and ruled in favor of the board members.[48]

Below: This fifty-five-thousand-gallon pressure tank car was manufactured by Union Tank in 1963. It was the largest tank car ever built by the company.

Opposite: A Union Tank employee inspects the truck, or undercarriage, of a tank car during the production process. As a member of The Marmon Group, Union Tank was peeled away from Trans Union into its own company.

The plaintiffs appealed, and on January 29, 1985, the Delaware Supreme Court, though upholding the lower court's decision, ruled three to two that the board had acted with haste when it approved the merger without first entertaining offers from other potential suitors and without obtaining valuation information to make an informed business decision.[49] Furthermore, the court held the board members personally responsible for the difference between the price paid by Marmon and the stock's "fair value."[50]

As Van Gorkom later told the *Chicago Tribune*, the court ignored "the fact that in that meeting the board did not decide to sell the company at $55. We couldn't sell the company. The shareholders make the ultimate decision. We voted to recommend the offer to the shareholders."[51]

"You know," Van Gorkom continued, "if somebody makes an error in logic, you try to correct it. But when somebody, especially a court of that kind of standing, displays such abysmal ignorance of the way the real world functions, and does something that is utterly incomprehensible, you hardly know where to start."[52]

The decision shook not only Van Gorkom and the rest of Trans Union's board but the entire corporate world. As Steinberg noted, "It meant that henceforth corporate directors would be held accountable for what were ruled to be 'bad corporate decisions.'"[53]

Bob Pritzker also remarked, "The decision was hailed by about forty law reviews to be one of the worst in business history. It was crazy."[54]

Though personally not involved in the matter, Jay was asked to intervene, primarily because he had an existing relationship with the plaintiffs' attorney, Bill Prickett. He agreed.

"Bill Prickett and I had been adversaries in a number of other suits," Jay explained. "Out of court we were warm friends. I said, 'Bill, you wove a tapestry out of nothing. You had no case, in my opinion, and you did a brilliant job of winning a verdict. This will break these guys. I want to settle.' He gave me a number. I gave him a number. We haggled."[55]

The settlement amount agreed upon was $23.5 million, which the high court approved on July 30, 1985. Trans Union's liability insurance covering its officers had a cap of $10 million, so Van Gorkom and the board members were responsible for the remaining $13.5 million.

Once again, however, Jay intervened. Because the settlement came four years after the merger, which was proving to be a very profitable one for Marmon, he agreed to pick up the $13.5 million bill, with one stipulation. Each of the board members was to donate twenty-five thousand dollars a year for five years to the Illinois Institute of Technology and the Stanford Medical School.

"The reason we paid the $13.5 million is because we thought the decision was unfair," said Bob Pritzker.

*The board hadn't done anything wrong and they were a very sophisticated board. One of the board members had been sick throughout this transaction, so why the court included him, I'll never figure out. Why did these people have to pay when they did nothing wrong and had nothing to gain? We felt we were the only people to gain from this, and we felt it was the only fair thing to do.*[56]

Through the charitable donation, the Pritzkers thought it was important to point out that they also had done nothing wrong. As Jay once remarked, "We wanted them to remember that this wasn't our responsibility. Everyone was happy with the result, and that was the end of it."[57]

---

In 1975, *BusinessWeek* magazine featured two sets of Pritzker brothers on its cover. By this time, the family had built one of the largest privately owned enterprises in the United States. Clockwise from left are A. N. Pritzker, Bob Pritzker, Jack Pritzker, and Jay Pritzker.

## The End of the Beginning

In many ways, the Trans Union acquisition marked the end of an era for The Marmon Group. With about $3 billion in sales by 1981, The Marmon Group had quickly grown into one of the largest private enterprises in the United States. Trans Union, responsible for about $1 billion of the revenue, was to be the last major acquisition for the next two decades. Yet The Marmon Group and its member companies would continue to grow, constantly seeking out smaller companies and good deals, consistently adding to their presence in a variety of industries.

The group of executives who would lead Marmon toward the new millennium was generally stable by the time the Trans Union deal closed. Bob Gluth would be Bob Pritzker's right-hand man. Similarly, George Jones remained deeply involved in company operations until his retirement in 1986. Yet the basic operating structure of The Marmon Group remained exceedingly lean, with the majority of the responsibility pushed down to the executives who ran individual member companies. Rather than as active micromanagers, the cadre of executives in Chicago viewed themselves as a consulting organization that provided tax, personnel, real estate, and other advice to the member companies of The Marmon Group.

It was a unique environment, remembered Carol D'Ascenzo, who joined The Marmon Group around the time of the Cerro acquisition. "I was going to be working for Walter Rogowski, general counsel at the Chicago office," she remembered. "My first impression was that this was a very unusual environment. Walter had a stand-up desk, but the first time I met him, he was lying on the floor, talking on the phone, with no shoes on."[58]

Chronicling the history of The Marmon Group is a little like taking a snapshot of a honeybee. The picture will represent only a single moment, presenting the illusion of stability when the reality is much more vibrant, illusory, and fast. The Marmon Group is nothing if not dynamic and difficult to define. From 1981 to 2001, Marmon Group member companies continued to grow and acquire and continued to expand across the spectrum of American industry. Section II illuminates the philosophical framework upon which The Marmon Group is built and then lists the companies, organized into arbitrary groupings.

1990: Albion Industries and the Shepherd companies join The Marmon Group.

1984: Altamil Corporation merger adds Fontaine companies to The Marmon Group.

1997: A busy year for acquisitions, especially medical products companies. Surgical Specialties, Manan Medical, and B. G. Sulzle join The Marmon Group.

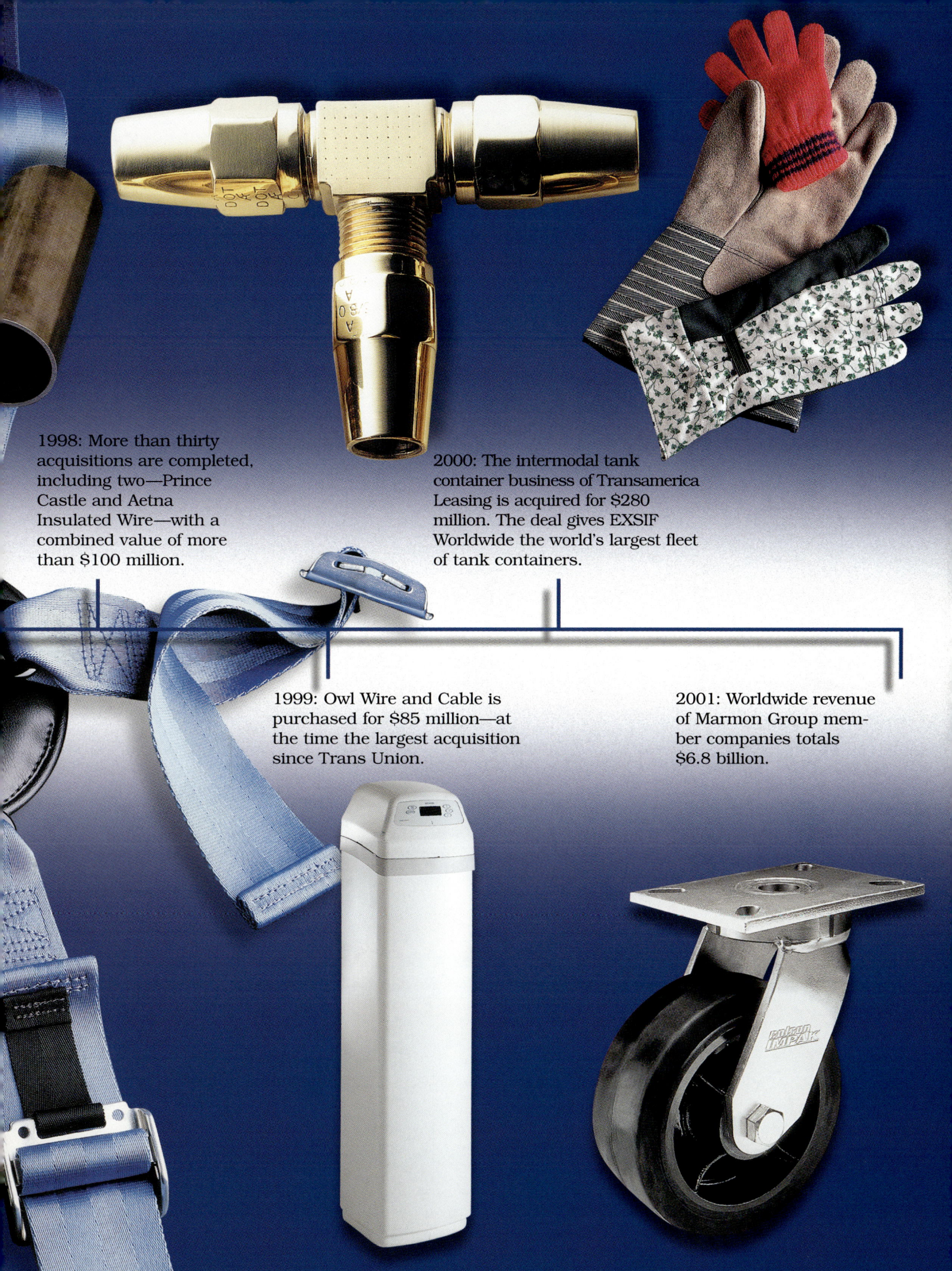

1998: More than thirty acquisitions are completed, including two—Prince Castle and Aetna Insulated Wire—with a combined value of more than $100 million.

1999: Owl Wire and Cable is purchased for $85 million—at the time the largest acquisition since Trans Union.

2000: The intermodal tank container business of Transamerica Leasing is acquired for $280 million. The deal gives EXSIF Worldwide the world's largest fleet of tank containers.

2001: Worldwide revenue of Marmon Group member companies totals $6.8 billion.

This Getz Bros. photo appeared in a Marmon Group brochure in 1995. By this time, Marmon boasted more than $6 billion in sales.

CHAPTER FIVE

# THE MARMON FRAMEWORK

*Trust is crucial in running this company.*

—Bob Pritzker, 2001

BY THE TIME THE TRANS UNION ACQUIsition closed, The Marmon Group had established a familiar pattern that would shift little over the next two decades. Under Bob Pritzker, The Marmon Group developed a list of official policies (there were only about fifteen) along with a cover letter that he gave to newly acquired companies. Between 1981 and 2001, the letter was never revised—a fact that fit in neatly with Bob's tendency for simplicity.

John Dolan, a Trans Union executive at the time his company joined The Marmon Group and later director of industrial relations for The Marmon Group, remarked on Pritzker's management style.

> *Bob used to teach at the University of Chicago, and he's more like a professor. When I came here, one vice president gave me some excellent advice. He told me to think of the office as patient waiting rooms and Bob is the doctor. He'll come around, and he doesn't like to read a lot of information. Don't send him long reports or any of those kinds of things. He'll come around and take your temperature and find out what's going on and how you feel and what he can do to help. It was good advice.[1]*

This is not to say, however, that The Marmon Group would remain static. Rather, the organization would always present a fluid and changing face to the business world. The only constants would be internal expansion and reinvestment augmented by a steady pace of acquisition, characterized more by opportunity than anything else. "Since Trans Union, my goal has been not to go into more fields," Bob Pritzker remarked in 2001. "We wanted to become stronger in the ones we're in and determine which ones we just should not be in because we don't need any more diversity. As a matter of fact, we get it by accident."[2]

Over the years, hundreds of millions of dollars were spent as companies joined The Marmon Group. Once acquired, companies were rarely divested. Marmon was in the position to invest in a company for the long term, patiently waiting while local management did what was best.

"There was no planned growth," remembered Bob Gluth, who joined The Marmon Group in 1969. "In Marmon, we're not planners, we're opportunists. We really haven't sat down and said, 'We really should get in this' and make a plan."[3]

Throughout the rapid growth, the staff in Chicago remained small, sometimes to the

---

Wells Lamont, one of the world's premier glove makers, is a Marmon Group member company. The Marmon Group's unique operating philosophy changed little from 1981 to 2001.

Bob Pritzker in the 1990s in Hungary at the wheel of a Russian-made tractor. Pritzker continued to travel relentlessly, visiting every member company every year.

consternation of outside sales people and consultants who saw Marmon's revenue estimates and called on the Chicago office expecting to find a large, stratified organization that might need a mainframe or a complex telephone system. Instead, what they found was a low-key, small group of executives, mostly accountants and other experts, who advised a multi-billion-dollar group of companies. Rather than managers, this group tended to view itself as acquisition scouts and consultants to Marmon's more than one hundred member companies.

"We don't think that our guys are better than the average in other companies," Bob Pritzker said. "We don't take the attitude that we are smarter than they are. Our people may be more technically knowledgeable in the law, for example, but they don't know nearly as much about the specific circumstances. We will give member companies guidance as a lawyer would give them guidance."[4]

Throughout the years, opportunities were constantly presented to the Pritzkers and other executives at Marmon, and for every company that was successfully bought, perhaps a dozen were considered and rejected. True to the precedent set by Jay Pritzker, Marmon moved on potential acquisitions with speed and surety, sending in small teams from Chicago to rapidly evaluate a company's potential and future. The team considered a lot of factors, including any potential liability, its financial health, morale, tax status, any potential environmental problems, and capacity for growth.

Raymond Avendt, as vice president of environmental activities of The Marmon Group, Inc., became part of the due diligence team. He joined The Marmon Group when his environmental consulting company was acquired in 1988 and has been assessing companies for acquisition ever since.

"What will happen is that there are certain factors that need to be evaluated in order to make a qualitative decision," Avendt said.

*Environmental liability needs to be quantified, labor relations, any legal liability, risk management, health and safety, plus the financial guys. We'll go in and kick the tires after the company has made the first purely financial cut. Do they have problems with OSHA? Do they have problems with the EPA? What's their debt? Is there any pending legal action? Every one of the people that are in different disciplines will have a chance to say, "Well, wait a minute."*[5]

Within this framework, Dolan, the retired director of industrial relations, compares Marmon's due diligence efforts to a "SWAT team."[6] The team moves quickly and thoroughly, presenting concise, decision-making information to Bob.

"Mr. Pritzker didn't like to read a lot of long, thick reports with trivia in them," Dolan said. "He really wanted to know what issues I might identify that would impact the purchase price. So if I saw something such as unfunded pension benefits or health care benefits, we would calculate the value of that to take it off the purchase price."[7]

This entire process might last only a couple of days, sometimes even less for smaller acquisitions. At the end of the due diligence, all of the various liabilities are considered against the revenue and a price is derived. "I might be gone for only two or three days looking at something," Gluth remembered. "But I'll make up my mind in a day."[8] In many cases, once Gluth had approved an acquisition, he would take the deal to Bob Pritzker, who had the ultimate say on any purchase.

The very speed of this process is one of the selling points. "We're prepared to act rapidly," said Bob Webb, who succeeded Walter Rogowski as senior vice president and general counsel of The Marmon Group, Inc. "We're a private company. We don't have seventeen layers of bureaucracy."[9]

One element that was never considered during due diligence was potential synergy with other Marmon Group companies; each Marmon Group company had to stand on its own as a successful enterprise. This, more than any other single factor, became the defining quality of the sprawling Marmon Group. While more traditional corporations organized themselves around concepts like "synergy" and "core competencies," The Marmon Group comprised member companies run by executives who were almost completely autonomous in their ability to make business decisions.

"I remember when I first got here," remarked David Dees, director of communications since 1998.

*I had been at a member company [L. A. Darling] for six years, so I knew that the individual businesses enjoyed a great deal of freedom. But when I came to work at the Chicago office, I was very quickly reminded that the philosophy of autonomy and local responsibility was not just talk. I think in my first week here, there were three cases in which I was contacted by newspaper reporters in far-flung cities—three incidents in which somebody called seeking information or comment. My instinct was to try to deal with it directly. Then it hit me that those responses are supposed to come from our member companies, not typically from the Chicago office unless it relates to The Marmon Group as a whole. Our job is to provide counsel to the companies when and where it's needed.*[10]

Marmon's reporting lines reflected this intense decentralization. Once a decision was made to buy a particular company, an offer was presented to the owners. If accepted, the company's financial reporting lines were established. Smaller companies that shared markets with and had been scouted out by larger Marmon Group companies often reported to the member company rather than to the Chicago office. Larger companies, however, would report directly to Bob Pritzker and his staff in Chicago. The Chicago office itself remained an almost invisible presence, although all member companies were charged an administrative services cost.

"We feel our member companies are like customers," said Bob Pritzker.

This general outline changed little over time. In 1998, however, Bob—already known for his great trust in his employees—delegated more responsibility to his vice presidents. That year alone, The Marmon Group negotiated thirty acquisitions. Still, Bob Pritzker maintained an ambitious global travel schedule, making sure he visited each member company at least once a year. His punishing schedule would often find him in three cities in one day and sometimes two or three countries in the course of a week.

### The Marmon Appeal

Companies joined The Marmon Group for many reasons. In many cases, the owners were ready to cash out, but they wanted to continue working. Marmon, which would often leave the existing management in place, was the perfect home. "On one acquisition, we had already given our pitch to the owner and we'd agreed to the deal," Pritzker said. "After it was done, during the finishing touches, I said, 'Why do you want to sell to us? Because on an IPO with an investment banker, you'll get more money.' He said, 'Because I want more capital to expand because I've got a bunch of ideas.' We told him to call any member company, and he did and they were enthusiastic. Everybody seems to trust us."[11]

Not surprisingly, the turnover among senior managers at Marmon member companies was exceedingly low.

Of course, not all companies join The Marmon Group for the access to capital. In some cases, a company might agree to sell because it was in trouble and sought new ownership to protect it from corporate raiders who would split a company for its assets.

Member company presidents reported that Bob Pritzker gave them great latitude to grow their companies. In Chicago, many of his senior executives were once employed at member companies, and they too reported that Pritzker trusted them completely to do their jobs.

Within the member companies, requests for investment that were accompanied by a compelling reason were rarely turned down. Moreover, each company has its own independent set of books and, although Marmon companies were allowed to work with each other, there was never any pressure to form supplier relationships that might not be the most efficient or economical options available. Supplier relationships that were created were often the result of networking at an annual meeting of member company general managers or through the Marmon College, a continuing education program for member companies.

"We put on a pretty wide variety of seminars," Dees said. "We cover environmental issues. We have a course called accounting for nonaccountants. Within the communications area, we put on a couple of seminars every year, including marketing communications and information technology. We often get some people from the member companies who have success stories to tell, and we bring in outside experts as well."[12]

As the number of companies grew and the complexity of the oversight increased, The Marmon Group identified segments of member companies. Like The Marmon Group itself, these categories were always changing in composition. But these shifts mattered little since the groupings were mostly arbitrary, arrived at for the sake of convenience when it came to publishing the annual brochure. They were no indication of a larger corporate strategy behind the organization.

In fact, The Marmon Group stubbornly resisted any kind of corporate organization as a matter of principle. This stance was driven by Bob Pritzker himself, who had an aversion to large bureaucracies. He reasoned that if the companies were lumped together into management and buying groups, The Marmon Group would need to hire a layer of vice presidents to oversee the groups. Of course, this new layer of vice presidents would need support staff, and most likely they would need to report to another layer of executive vice presidents, who themselves would need support staff. Pritzker envisioned this process multiplying out of control until he found himself ensconced in a highly inefficient and political web. He preferred to keep things as simple and direct as possible.

The people who worked for Bob Pritzker, especially those who had been at the company for many years, developed a great deal of respect for his openness, his ability to ask the right questions, and his sense of trust in his subordinates.

"Trust is crucial in running this company," Pritzker said. "If the people don't believe in us, don't believe that I'll tell them the truth, that I'll answer a question correctly, and that we have a high level of integrity, then nobody is going to cooperate with us. If somebody isn't forthright from this office, I'll call the other person and say, 'Look, we didn't give you the right answer.' I just won't put up with that, and I think everybody knows it."[13]

Bob Webb, Marmon's longtime general counsel, remembered what it was like to move from Beatrice, a large publicly traded company, to Marmon's office. "It was like a breath of fresh air," Webb said. "I had the freedom, the flexibility to do things. The biggest change from Beatrice was the immediacy of everything. There's no tomorrow. There's yesterday and this morning. You just get in and roll up your sleeves and do what you can in the time allotted. Bob Pritzker is the exact opposite of a micromanager."[14]

The ultimate test of this unique approach to running a business is, of course, whether it works—and in that sense The Marmon Group has compiled an irrefutable case. Its member companies have become world-leading suppliers of products including airplane seat belts, casters, and pipe and tubing, among others. In most cases, these positions weren't obtained via acquisition, but rather they were developed by individual member companies through their life span in The Marmon Group.

## The Future of The Marmon Group

By 2000, The Marmon Group had grown into an immense organization, with annual sales of its member companies at around $6.8 billion and profit of $300 million. And still the enterprise was growing. In 2000 alone, Marmon Group member companies completed more than twenty acquisitions, bringing the number to more than fifty for a three-year period. One of the acquisitions that year, a $280 million deal for the intermodal tank container business of Transamerica Leasing, was the largest acquisition since Trans Union. In all, that year's investment in acquisitions stood at $500 million. Like many of Marmon's more recent acquisitions, these new targets were often brought to Pritzker's attention by member companies, so they complemented existing Marmon Group companies in industries including retail display, intermodal tank containers, consumer credit information, fasteners, and metal products. Within the existing Marmon Group, member companies built or expanded more than twenty facilities in 2000.

In 2001, Marmon concluded some rather uncharacteristic divestitures. Among the companies sold were two longtime member companies, Jamesway, a producer of poultry incubator/hatcher systems, and Long-Airdox, a global manufacturer of underground coal-mining equipment.

Through these sales, Marmon was effectively focusing on fewer and more defined business segments. Major growth areas in recent years included wire and cable products and medical devices, while tank car leasing and consumer credit information remained by far the largest business segments. But the concentration of resources into particular industries had little effect on the overall Marmon operating principles of nearly complete autonomy, trust, simplicity, and effective leadership at the local level. Whether it augured anything for the future remained to be seen.

In the meantime, however, The Marmon Group of 2001 was very much like The Marmon Group of 1981—except that it had grown much larger. The company was indelibly imprinted with the personality and operating principles of Bob Pritzker, who started as a young engineer bettering Colson's antiquated operation in Elyria, Ohio, and presided over the growth of one of America's largest privately owned enterprises.

Through steady investment, Trans Union's credit reporting business has grown to be the largest in the United States.

CHAPTER SIX

# SERVICES

## CONSUMER PRODUCTS, MARKETING, AND FINANCIAL SERVICES

Getz Bros. & Co., Inc.
MarCap Companies
Beijing Huilian Food Co., Ltd.
Wells Lamont Corporation

## CREDIT DATA AND INFORMATION MANAGEMENT

Trans Union LLC

# Consumer Products, Marketing, and Financial Services

The Marmon Group is active in a variety of businesses in consumer products, marketing, and financial services. Through Getz Bros., which joined The Marmon Group as part of the 1981 Trans Union deal, Marmon operates the United States' largest noncommodity marketing and distribution firm. Wells Lamont, a 1977 acquisition, is a well-known maker of gloves. Other companies include a financing business and a Chinese maker of baby food.

### Getz Bros. & Co., Inc.

Getz Bros. is the United States' largest noncommodity international marketing and distribution firm.[1] After joining The Marmon Group in 1981, it was immediately fine-tuned by Bob, who streamlined the business, disposing of untidy odds and ends, and strengthened Getz's management and financial controls.[2]

For example, as Marmon's former director of communications, Jack Steinberg, reported, "Its branch in Japan switched from eclectic promotion of whatever it could sell, to specialized marketing of heart pacemakers and other cardiovascular and related medical devices. It became a runaway success, earning as much as all other Getz branches in Asia."[3]

Getz got its start in California in 1858, when a twenty-two-year-old immigrant from Prussia named Joseph Getz founded the first general store in what is now Lake County.[4] By the early 1880s Getz Bros. was exporting canned and cured foods to customers in Shanghai, Hong Kong, Calcutta, and Madras. After Joseph Getz died in 1896, his brother Louis sailed to Asia to add to the firm's list of international trading partners. This expedition led to the opening three years later of the first Getz overseas office in Shanghai.[5]

Getz's long history of expansion has continued since it became a member of The Marmon Group. A historic acquisition occurred in August 1989, when Getz became the first American company to buy 100 percent ownership of a Hungarian firm. The acquisition of Intercooperation Company, a major Budapest-based trading concern, was made possible after the Hungarian government changed its laws about foreign ownership.[6]

In 1986, Getz purchased a general trading company in Thailand, Louis T. Leonowens (Thai) Ltd. The company was established in 1905 by the son of Anna Leonowens, the British woman whose life story, *Anna and the King of Siam*, was the inspiration for the musical *The King and I*.

Getz's diverse offerings of international trading and marketing services now include the following groups:

• Biomedical Products: Regional teams of marketing, sales, clinical, licensing, administrative, and

Both pages: Getz Bros., which joined The Marmon Group at the time of the Trans Union acquisition, was founded in 1858 by a Prussian immigrant named Joseph Getz, one of the men in the photo at left. As a Marmon member company, Getz has grown into the country's largest noncommodity international marketing and distribution firm.

data systems professionals represent Western manufacturers in Asian and Pacific markets.

• Consumer Products: With more than one hundred years of experience marketing packaged foods and consumer products overseas, Getz continues to build brands and move products in Europe, the Far East, and the Pacific. Brand names associated overseas with Getz have included Borden, Heineken, Gallo, Heinz, Perrier, Quaker Oats, Pacesetter, St. Jude, Baxter, Armstrong, Upjohn, Massey-Ferguson, Black & Decker, Eastman Kodak, Maidenform, and Helene Curtis.

• Technical/Industrial Products: Materials-handling systems, tools, and specialty chemicals are among the diverse products that Getz Bros. has marketed internationally.[7]

• Information Technology Division: Getz develops its own software programs as well as distributing selected software imported from United States and European suppliers.

• Commercial Interiors: This group helps manufacturers access the market for commercial interior products in developing international business capitals such as Bangkok, Taipei, Budapest, and Hong Kong, as well as in European commercial centers.

Today the Chicago-based firm has offices or representative offices in Australia, China, New Zealand, Hungary, Japan, the Philippines, Singapore, Pakistan, South Africa, Thailand, Vietnam, Malaysia, the United Kingdom, Latvia, Estonia, Taiwan, Lithuania, and Poland, as well as the United States. Getz Bros. has approximately sixteen hundred employees.[8]

---

A pacemaker marketed by Getz Bros. Getz distributes and markets a wide variety of products in 20 countries.

## MarCap Companies

MarCap is essentially a financing company that specializes in leasing medical and other high-tech equipment, including commercial aircraft. It also has an equity position in a fleet of boats, the Candy Fleet, serving the oil and gas industry in the Gulf of Mexico.[9] Its focus, however, is the financing of medical equipment, primarily diagnostic, used in hospitals, clinics, and outpatient imaging centers around the country.[10]

Headquartered in Chicago, MarCap employs 245 people.

## Beijing Huilian Food Co., Ltd.

The Marmon Group increased its business activity in China with the 1998 acquisition of 89.9 percent of Beijing Huilian Food Company, a producer and marketer of baby food.[11] Historically, Chinese babies have been raised on a diet of rice and noodles. Since beginning operations in 1997, Beijing Huilian has become a leading jarred-baby-food company in China. Its thirteen varieties of jarred food, including carrots, liver, chicken, apples, and peaches, are sold through major supermarkets and department stores located in seventy-three cities.[12] It has 110 employees and recently built a new factory.

## Wells Lamont Corporation

Obtained by The Marmon Group with the 1977 acquisition of the Hammond Corporation, Wells Lamont was the deal's real prize. It blossomed into the world's largest manufacturer of gloves,[13] with more than 1 million square feet of manufacturing and distribution facilities that employ more than 4,000 people in the United States and abroad.[14]

# CHAPTER SIX: SERVICES

The firm, based in Niles, Illinois, makes numerous brands and a wide range of gloves for work, garden, recreation, dress, industry, and even for use in space. In December 1993, Wells Lamont's cut-resistant glove liners, typically worn by surgeons to minimize the risk of cuts during surgical procedures, were on board the space shuttle *Endeavour* and were worn by astronauts underneath their pressurized gloves while they repaired the Hubble telescope.[15]

That's many years and many miles from the company's founding in 1907, when W. O. Wells, a twenty-four-year-old jobber of buggy whips and hosiery in Aberdeen, South Dakota, thought he saw a market for work gloves. With an initial investment of five hundred dollars, Wells bought five sewing machines, fashioned patterns for canvas, cotton, and leather work and dress gloves, and then hired ten local women to make them.[16]

The early success of Wells's business, however, was due as much to his ability to follow as to his ability to lead. He was a man who made quality products, and he always demanded cash on delivery. But one of his earliest customers was a Wyoming-based retailer of general merchandise who insisted on paying net thirty days after the gloves' delivery to his small chain of ten stores. Wells decided to change his cash-only policy, and he and J. C. Penney did business continuously thereafter. Within a few years, Wells was selling his gloves nationwide.[17] Needing help, in 1914 Wells took on a partner, his lifelong friend Maurice Lamont, and renamed the company Wells Lamont. Only six months later, Lamont was killed in a hunting

Above and below: A selection of Wells Lamont gloves from Marmon Group annual brochures. Almost one hundred years old, Wells Lamont has been a prestigious name in the glove industry since its founding.

accident, but the company kept Lamont's name to honor him.[18]

Today, Wells Lamont operates three units or divisions: Austins Marmon makes a wide variety of gloves for other Wells Lamont business units and markets products in Asia; the Wells Lamont Europe Industrial division makes, markets, and distributes work gloves to the industrial trade for the United Kingdom and European markets; and Wells Lamont USA manufactures and markets gloves to industrial and retail markets in North America, including work, garden, medical, cut-resistant, clean-room and other special-needs products.[19]

## CREDIT DATA AND INFORMATION MANAGEMENT

The 1981 acquisition of Trans Union Corporation included a credit reporting business comprising assorted regional credit bureaus. After two decades of internal investment and acquisitions, Trans Union is a leading international information management company.

### Trans Union LLC

Even if consumers don't know the Trans Union name, they depend on the company's services for prompt access to credit. Trans Union maintains one of the world's largest databases of consumer credit information. Its products include credit reports, credit and insurance risk-scoring models, electronic decision systems, target marketing systems, and preemployment evaluation reports. The firm operates worldwide through a 275-member network of company-owned offices and independent credit bureaus that have approximately 3,600 employees.[20]

Headquartered in Chicago, Trans Union has company-owned or affiliated offices in all fifty states, plus locations in Canada, Botswana, Chile, China, Costa Rica, Kenya, Mexico, Namibia, Puerto Rico, South Africa, Australia, Colombia, the Czech Republic, Guatemala, India, Italy, South Korea, Swaziland, Thailand, Zimbabwe, and Honduras.[21]

Trans Union's most recent expansion has taken it into Thailand. In November 2000, the firm took a minority ownership position in Central Information System Company, a credit information bureau comprising thirteen of the leading Thai financial institutions.[22] This move followed the 1999 purchase of a majority interest in Credit Information Services, the largest consumer credit bureau in Hong Kong.[23]

Opposite: Trans Union LLC maintains one of the world's largest databases of consumer credit information.

TransUnion

An L. A. Darling retail display system. L. A. Darling is the oldest and largest of The Marmon Group's retail services companies.

CHAPTER SEVEN

# INDUSTRY

### Retail Services
L. A. Darling Company
Streater, Inc.
Thorco Industries, Inc.
Leader Metal Industry Co., Ltd.
Store Opening Solutions, Inc.
Prince Castle, Inc.
The Sloane Group

### Construction Products and Services
Meyer Material Company
Sterling Crane

### Industrial Products and Services
Atlas Bolt & Screw Company
Robertson, Inc.
Pan American Screw, Inc.
Nylok Fastener Corporation
Dynamic Logic, Ltd.
Amarillo Gear Company
Solidstate Controls, Inc.
Uni-Form Components Co.
Enersul, Inc.
Koehler-Bright Star, Inc.

### Pipe and Tube Distribution
Marmon/Keystone Corporation
Bushwick Metals, Inc.
Huron Steel Company, Inc.
Future Metals, Inc.

### Casters
Albion Industries, Inc., Colson Caster Corporation, and Shepherd Caster Corporation
Industrias Metalicas Sudamericanas, S.A.
Shepherd Products, Inc.
Shepherd Hardware Products, Ltd.

## Retail Services

Beginning with the acquisition of L. A. Darling in 1960, Marmon Group member companies have grown to provide equipment and services to the retail market and restaurant industry worldwide. In the fall of 2001, a Taiwan-based manufacturer of retail-display and food-service equipment joined the Group.

### L. A. Darling Company

Since its founding in 1897, L. A. Darling has been a leader in the retail merchandising industry. That tradition has continued since Bob and Jay Pritzker acquired the firm in 1960.

Based in Paragould, Arkansas, Darling and its Canadian affiliate operate six manufacturing and warehousing facilities totaling more than 1.9 million square feet and employing more than 1,600 people in Arkansas, Wisconsin, and Quebec. The company provides comprehensive retail display products and services to leading retail stores and brand marketers worldwide. In addition to its expansion and development, Darling has brought several other businesses into The Marmon Group since 1990.

L. A. Darling's product displays serve leading retailers worldwide.

### Streater, Inc.

In 2000, Darling purchased Streater Store Fixtures, a manufacturer of metal and wood store fixtures and permanent point-of-purchase displays. Founded in 1917 and based in Albert Lea, Minnesota, Streater employs 435 people and operates three adjacent manufacturing and warehousing facilities that total 568,400 square feet.[1]

### Thorco Industries, Inc.

Thorco Industries, of Lamar, Missouri, was acquired in 1990. Founded in 1899, Thorco designs and manufactures point-of-purchase displays as well as store fixtures from wire, sheet metal, and tubing.

The company's three plants in the southwest Missouri communities of Lamar, Butler, and Cassville, and an affiliated company's factory in Santa Ana, Mexico, total 621,000 square feet and employ about 660 workers.[2] Thorco in turn has grown with recent acquisitions of its own: NHD Group, an Ontario manufacturer of barbecue wire grids, material-handling containers, and point-of-purchase displays, has facilities totaling 118,000 square feet and employing 100 people. Unarco Industries in Wagoner, Oklahoma, a major supplier of plastic and wire shopping carts for discount and grocery stores, has a 500,000-square-foot plant and 400 employees.[3]

## Leader Metal Industry Co., Ltd.

Leader Metal Industry Co., Ltd., joined The Marmon Group in 2001.[4] Headquartered in Taipei, Taiwan, the company's manufacturing operations are located in Zhongshan, Guangdong Province, China. Leader manufactures wire and metal products including shelving, store fixture accessories, food-service equipment, material handling equipment, and more. The company employs 1,200 and has physical facilities totaling 487,500 square feet.[5]

## Store Opening Solutions, Inc.

Store Opening Solutions provides such store-opening services as project management, retail outfitting, logistics, warehousing, and distribution. The firm operates a 321,000-square-foot distribution center in Murfreesboro, Tennessee.[6] Store Opening Solutions has 50 employees.

## Prince Castle, Inc.

Acquired in 1998, Prince Castle is a leading manufacturer of specialty equipment for the commercial food-service industry.

Founded in 1956 to serve the rapidly developing fast-food business, the Carol Stream, Illinois, firm manufactures and distributes electronic, holding, and processing equipment for major fast-food restaurant chains.

Prince Castle's products include specialized timers and computers, hot-food holding cabinets, and toasters, as well as a variety of manual food-processing tools such as tomato slicers and other implements.[7] Prince Castle employs 250 people at its 123,000-square-foot plant in Carol Stream.

In 1999, the firm added a broad line of refrigeration equipment to its offerings when it acquired the Minneapolis-based Stevens-Lee Company, which designs and manufactures refrigeration equipment for many of the top restaurant chains.[8] Stevens-Lee has a 116,000-square-foot plant and 120 employees.

In 2000, Prince Castle expanded its market abroad when it announced the opening of an office in Paris as well as the purchase of two businesses located southeast of Paris in Bouilly—Catequip S.A. and Cat'Serv S.a.r.l. Both companies provide sales and service representation in Europe for North American food-service manufacturers.[9] Combined employment is 35 people.

A Prince Castle hot-food holder, left, and restaurant-grade toaster, right

## The Sloane Group

Founded in 1962 in London, The Sloane Group joined The Marmon Group in early 2001. The company manufactures a wide variety of merchandising systems, point-of-purchase displays, and furniture for retail stores, banks, and automobile showrooms. Employment totals 400.

Sloane's products are shipped throughout Europe, the Middle East, and Asia. With a wood factory in Wellingborough, England, a metal factory in Mildenhall, England, and distribution centers in Hungary, Poland, and the Czech Republic, Sloane's facilities cover about 200,000 square feet.

## CONSTRUCTION PRODUCTS AND SERVICES

Marmon Group member companies provide a variety of products and services for construction. Meyer Material provides ready-mix concrete and related construction materials and services, while Sterling Crane rents cranes for industrial maintenance and construction.

### Meyer Material Company

Meyer Material joined The Marmon Group in 1983. In January 2000, Meyer expanded through acquisition, bringing its total number of concrete plants to 23.

Based in McHenry, Illinois, Meyer Material has been associated with The Marmon Group since 1959. In 1983, it became a member.[10]

Ben Meyer founded the firm in the early 1920s as the Meyer Coal & Material Company. His business grew along with the booming Chicago region after World War II as the United States experienced a period of rapid growth.

In 1959, Meyer sold the firm. It has grown considerably through a combination of both new construction and acquisitions. Today, Meyer Material's principal business is the production and supply of ready-mixed concrete for a variety of construction projects, including residential, commercial, industrial, and public works.[11]

After acquiring in January 2000 the assets of five other ready-mix concrete operations also located in the northwestern suburbs of Chicago, Meyer has a total of twenty-three concrete plants and ten sand and gravel plants and operates a fleet of 475 ready-mix concrete trucks. The firm's facilities now cover nearly 2,500 acres and employ 700 people.[12]

Meyer also acquired Paveloc Industries, Inc., which manufactures concrete paving stones and retaining wall systems. Paveloc is based in Marengo, Illinois, and operates from a 53,000-square-foot, completely automated plant. The company has 30 employees.

### Sterling Crane

When Sterling Crane joined The Marmon Group in 1982, the company operated a fleet of 290 cranes for industrial maintenance and construction. Now, Sterling owns and operates more than 400 hydraulic and conventional boom mobile cranes, one of the largest and most modern fleets

Sterling Crane operates one of the largest fleets of hydraulic and conventional boom mobile cranes in Canada.

CHAPTER SEVEN: INDUSTRY

in Canada. Headquartered in Edmonton, Alberta, Sterling Crane supplies cranes from fourteen branches throughout western Canada and employs 365 people. In addition to providing equipment and service for its own cranes, the company erects and dismantles tower cranes (the type used on top of buildings) that are not part of its fleet. Sterling's equipment is used to lift almost anything too heavy or awkward to lift by hand, from signs to refinery vessels weighing hundreds of tons.

Sterling traces its roots to the opening of the first branch in Regina, Saskatchewan, in 1964. In 1972, the company combined with Hulburd's Crane Service, which was founded in Edmonton in 1954.

## INDUSTRIAL PRODUCTS AND SERVICES

Marmon's operations in industrial products represent a diverse group of companies, from makers of right-angle gears, lighting equipment, and power-supply systems to manufacturers of fasteners.

### Atlas Bolt & Screw Company

Founded in 1896, Atlas manufactures and engineers a complete line of thread-cutting, thread-forming, self-drilling, and self-tapping fasteners in carbon and stainless steel, used in the construction market for metal-to-metal, metal-to-wood, and masonry applications.[13]

Due to acquisitions as well as internal growth, Atlas has grown considerably since the Trans Union merger in 1981.

In 1991, for example, Atlas bought two complementary firms—West Coast Fasteners in Oregon and Guardian Fastener & Closure Systems in Pennsylvania—which had the effect of increasing Atlas's product lines and markets by a full two-thirds.[14] In 1998, Atlas grew even more with the purchase of the Co-Op

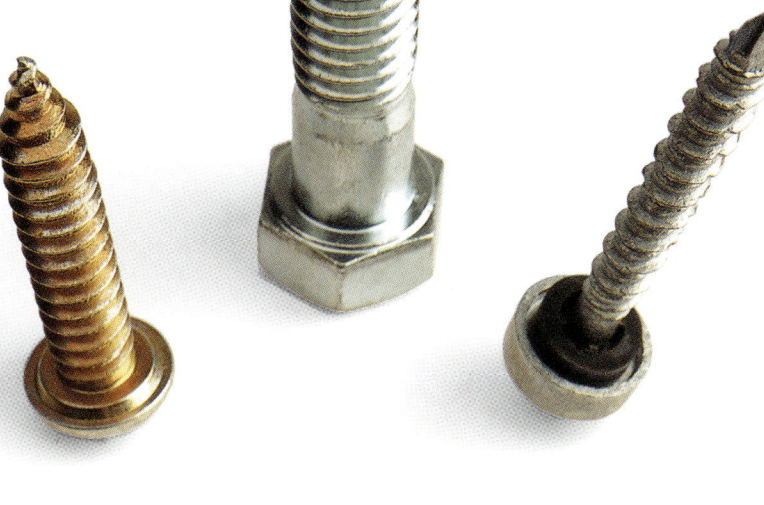

Fasteners from Marmon Group member companies, including Atlas Bolt & Screw Company; Robertson, Inc.; and Nylok Fastener Corporation, which was acquired in 2000.

Screw Manufacturing Corporation in New Jersey.[15] Based in Ashland, Ohio, Atlas now has facilities in Georgia, New Jersey, North Carolina, Oregon, and Texas, as well as in China, Poland, and Sweden. It has a total of 279,000 square feet of manufacturing and warehouse space and has 450 employees.[16]

### Robertson, Inc.

Robertson, Inc., manufactures industrial fasteners, standards, and specials in steel, stainless, and non-ferrous materials. Headquartered in Milton, Ontario, the company is also a specialty manufacturer of collated screws and industrial power and hand screwdrivers. It joined The Marmon Group during the 1981 Trans Union acquisition.

In addition to its Canadian operations, Robertson has a plant in Zhjiang, China. The company's facilities cover a total of 160,000 square feet and employ 125 people. An affiliated company, Specialty Bolt & Stud,[17] distributes stainless steel fasteners as well as structural threaded rods, studs, nuts, and bolts. Also located in Milton, Ontario, the business has a 25,000-square-foot plant and 25 employees.[18]

### Pan American Screw, Inc.

Also acquired via the Trans Union acquisition, Pan American Screw, Inc., distributes industrial fasteners, standards, and specials in various materials for industrial and commercial distributors, mail order, and retail sales to independent lumber and hardware stores. Other products include collated screws and screwdrivers.

Based in Conover, North Carolina, Pan American has operations in the United States and Mexico totaling 57,000 square feet and employing 55 people.

### Nylok Fastener Corporation

Based in Macomb, Michigan, Nylok became a member of The Marmon Group in 2000. The company manufactures a variety of fasteners that lock, seal, and protect threads through a patented process. Nylok-treated nuts, screws, bolts, and special fasteners can be found in a variety of industries, including aerospace and consumer electronics.

Nylok operates through twenty-two licensees in sixteen countries, as well as having an operation in Canada. The company employs 230, and total square footage is 190,000.

### Dynamic Logic, Ltd.

Dynamic Logic designs and manufactures a full line of remote monitoring equipment, known as telemetry outstations and loggers, for the water and wastewater industries. Headquartered in Dartford, England, with a manufacturing facility in Fife, Scotland, Dynamic has 140 employees and 43,600 total square feet.

### Amarillo Gear Company

Founded in 1935 in Amarillo, Texas—in the heart of the Dust Bowl—Amarillo Gear was a major manufacturer of right-angle gear drives for agricultural irrigation pumps when it became a Marmon Group member in 1964.[19] But because the business was seasonal, Amarillo Gear began to round out its product line by producing right-angle gear drives for cooling tower fans and other types of vertical machines, such as agitators, mixers, dryers, and separators. In the 1970s, the firm took its advanced gear technology into a new market by establishing the Exeter, California, Amarillo Wind Machine Company. Amarillo Wind produces and installs wind machines that help protect fruits and vegetables from frost damage by circulating cold ground-level air and displacing it with warmer air from above.[20]

Today, Amarillo Gear manufactures and distributes the world's most extensive line of right-angle spiral-bevel gears in its Texas facility. Combined, Amarillo Gear and Amarillo Wind Machine employ 170 people at plants totaling 138,000 square feet.[21]

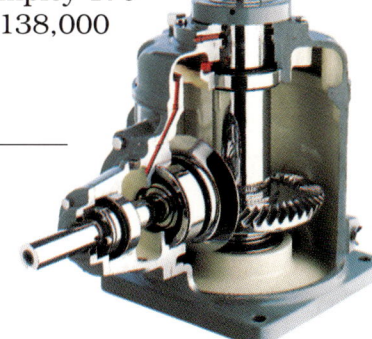

Amarillo Gear Company manufactures the world's largest line of right-angle spiral-bevel gears.

## Solidstate Controls, Inc.

Solidstate Controls, a pioneer in high-performance Uninterruptible Power Supply (UPS) systems, came into the Marmon fold in 1981 during the Trans Union merger.

UPS systems are designed to convert battery power into usable power. They also smooth spikes of incoming current.[22] A small sampling of Solidstate's UPS-system customers includes power generating plants, chemical and processing companies, and original equipment manufacturers.[23]

With a manufacturing plant and headquarters in Columbus, Ohio, Solidstate markets its products worldwide. In 1994, the firm established an office in Hong Kong and created networks of independent sales representatives in Asia and Latin America. In 1999, JCB Electronica Industrial SRL, an Argentina-based manufacturer of UPS systems and cathodic protection systems, was acquired. It has since changed its name to Solidstate Controls, Inc. de Argentina SRL. Solidstate also has an office in Mexico. Total square footage is about 70,000, and the company employs more than 200 people.

An affiliated company, HDR Power Systems, Inc., manufactures power electronic equipment for industrial heating. Also located in Columbus, Ohio, HDR has an 18,500-square-foot plant and 20 employees.[24]

## Uni-Form Components Co.

A member of The Marmon Group since 1994, Uni-Form Components manufactures standard and customized tank heads and other components from steel, stainless steel, aluminum, and other metals, in sizes up to seventy-five feet in diameter and a thickness of seven inches. Its products serve the petrochemical, rail transportation, aerospace, hydrocarbon processing, and oil and gas industries. Based in Houston, Texas, Uni-Form Components has 90 employees.[25]

## Enersul, Inc.

Based in Calgary, Alberta, Enersul specializes in the design, manufacture, and operation of sulfur processing and handling plants that convert this by-product of oil and natural gas processing into a form that can be transported safely.[26] Although sulfur, called brimstone in biblical times, is used to make gunpowder and matches, its greatest application today is as a phosphate fertilizer building block.[27]

Enersul was founded in 1952 under the name of Vennard & Ellithorpe (V&E). In 1972, V&E became Procor Sulfur Services Inc., after being acquired by Procor Limited. In 1981, the company joined The Marmon Group during the Trans Union merger and became Procor Sulfur Services. After the purchase of Tiger Industries, a manufacturer of sulfur-based fertilizers, and a major reorganization in 1998, the company was renamed Enersul Inc.[28] It offers general management services for its primary operations: Enersul Operations, Enersul Technologies, Tiger Industries, and Tiger-Sunbelt Industries.[29]

In addition to the plants it operates in North America, Enersul has designed, built, and sold other sulfur forming and handling plants in various parts of the world, including Asia, the Middle East, Africa, and Europe.[30] The company employs 250 people.

Right: Enersul, Inc., provides services, products, and technology for processing and distributing sulfur. The sulfur business was part of Trans Union at the time of the 1981 acquisition.

### Koehler-Bright Star, Inc.

Koehler-Bright Star produces specialized portable lighting equipment, including battery-powered cap lamps, flashlights and lanterns, and flame safety lamps, in addition to batteries and charging equipment used in mining, tunneling, fire fighting, utility, and industrial safety.[31]

Olympic Games officials have also relied upon the company's products since 1980. According to Olympic tradition, the games begin with the lighting of a torch using a flame brought from Mount Olympus in Greece. After being carried down the mountain, the flame is put on a plane and flown to the country hosting the Games. In 1996, the Olympic committee used a Koehler lamp to keep the flame alive as it was flown to Los Angeles before beginning its cross-country trek to Atlanta.[32]

Koehler-Bright Star was formed after the Koehler Manufacturing Company, founded in 1912 and a Marmon Group member since 1996, acquired Bright Star Industries in 1998; the two companies merged to increase product lines and efficiency.[33] Based in Wilkes-Barre, Pennsylvania, the firm's 115,000-square-foot facility employs 110 people.

Above: A Koehler-Bright Star miner's cap lamp. Koehler-Bright Star provides a variety of portable lighting equipment, including the lamp used to transport the Olympic flame from Greece to the host country.

# CHAPTER SEVEN: INDUSTRY

## PIPE AND TUBE DISTRIBUTION

Marmon Group member companies distribute specialty pipe and tubing in a wide variety of metals, including steel, carbon, aluminum, and various other alloys, for use in many industries and businesses worldwide. In fact, Marmon/Keystone Corporation is the largest distributor of specialty pipe and tubing.

### Marmon/Keystone Corporation

Marmon/Keystone can be traced back to 1907, when William Horwitz, an eager young man who felt confined in his family's general-store business, pooled resources with two partners to purchase a small oil well supply store in Butler, Pennsylvania, for six hundred dollars. The store, called Keystone Pipe & Supply, sold new and used pipe in the rapidly developing oil fields of western Pennsylvania.[34]

Among the Pritzkers' many deals, the purchase of Keystone ranks among the best. When this steel pipe and tubing distributor joined The Marmon Group in 1970, it had seven distribution centers in the United States. Today, it has more than fifty sales and service centers throughout the United States, Canada, Mexico, the United Kingdom, and Europe.[35]

With an inventory of more than ten thousand sizes and grades of carbon, aluminum, and stainless steel pipe and tubing, in addition to bar products in chrome, stainless, and nitro steel, Marmon/Keystone has become one of the largest distributors of specialty tubular and bar products anywhere in the world.[36] Its total physical facilities occupy more than 3.2 million square feet and employ 1,300 people.[37]

Although expansion of its original facilities played a role, the company's growth was also fueled by acquisitions in the 1990s. For example, in 1994 Marmon/Keystone purchased Specialty Steels, a distributor of stainless steel fluid handling, structural, and metal fastener products based in Canada. Its first European acquisition came in 1995, when it purchased the Anbuma Group, a Belgian distributor of pipe and tube.[38] In 1996, it bought Florida-based Future Metals, a distributor of aircraft tubing and specialty parts. And in 1997, the firm acquired the Wheeler Group, a pipe and tube distributor based in England.[39]

Domestically, most of Marmon/Keystone's product is delivered to its customers by its internal fleet of trucks. Marmon/Keystone also operates a subsidiary trucking company, M/K Express, established in 1986.[40]

### Bushwick Metals, Inc.

Bushwick Metals, a Marmon/Keystone acquisition based in Bridgeport, Connecticut, distributes carbon steel products, including structural shapes, plate and sheet, bars, and tubing. Bushwick Metals has 135 employees, and its facilities total more than 500,000 square feet. Azco Steel Company, a division of Bushwick, distributes heavy structural, plate, and wide-flange beams.

### Huron Steel Company, Inc.

Acquired in 1972 as part of the American Steel & Pump deal, Huron Steel, based in Detroit, Michigan, is a service center specializing in the distribution of cold-drawn carbon and alloy bars.[41] The firm's warehouse facility covers 58,000 square feet and employs 25 people.[42]

### Future Metals, Inc.

Future Metals is a leading distributor of aircraft-grade tubing, rolled-form shapes, and other raw material to some of the largest aerospace companies in the world, including Boeing and General Electric.[43] Founded in 1971, it joined The Marmon Group in 1996. The company stocks more than seven thousand different products, which are used in various parts of both commercial and cargo airplanes.[44]

Based in Fort Lauderdale, Florida, Future Metals has about 100 employees, and the company operates distribution centers in Cerritos, California; Commack, New York; Arlington, Texas; Pacific, Washington; Gorinchem, Holland; and Southampton, England. The company's facilities have a total square footage of about 140,000.

## CASTERS

Considered together, Marmon Group member companies lead the world in caster production. These companies sell into all different caster markets—from consumer to industrial—worldwide.

### Albion Industries, Inc., Colson Caster Corporation, and Shepherd Caster Corporation

Albion, Colson, and Shepherd are operated as separate companies, but if they were combined, the resulting firm would constitute the largest manufacturer of casters in the world.[45]

Albion Industries of Albion, Michigan, which joined Marmon in 1990, manufactures light- to super-duty casters and wheels with capacities from fifty to one hundred thousand pounds to serve a wide range of industries. Its light- and medium-duty line, for example, is used for hotel and institutional equipment such as laundry trucks and food service racks. Heavy-duty casters are made for automobile body dollies and aircraft cargo-handling equipment. In addition, Albion produces high-capacity casters for several unusual applications, including revolving restaurants and the space shuttle's fuel cells at Cape Canaveral, Florida. With 131,000 square feet of production and warehouse space, Albion has 160 employees.[46]

In 1953, Bob and Jay Pritzker purchased the Colson Company, which at the time made casters, bicycles, and hospital equipment, as well as Mighty Mouse rockets for the navy. Today it manufactures some thirty-five thousand different casters, wheels, and rubber bumpers for industrial, institutional, and commercial equipment. Headquartered in Jonesboro, Arkansas, Colson also has facilities in Canada and Mexico, for a total of 304,100 square feet and 590 employees. Colson increased its presence and capacity in Canada with the 1999 purchase of Conestogo Plastics. Founded in 1979, Conestogo manufactures custom products such as casters, garden tools, appliance parts, and garage door rollers.[47] Conestogo and Colson plants in Monette, Arkansas, and Gallatin, Tennessee, constitute the Colson Plastics Division, which manufactures caster wheels as well as custom molded commercial and industrial products.

The Colson name also has a significant presence overseas. Colson Caster Guangzhou manufactures custom casters for industrial,

---

Above: Shepherd and Albion casters. Both companies joined The Marmon Group in 1990.

Opposite: A Colson thermo plastic total lock caster brake, designed to stop casters from rolling unexpectedly. When its caster businesses are considered in the aggregate, The Marmon Group is the world's leading manufacturer of casters.

institutional, and commercial equipment in Yonghe, China, in a 33,570-square-foot facility that employs 90 workers.[48]

Based in England and serving the European market, Colson Europe manufactures wheels and casters for institutional and industrial applications. With 200,000 square feet of manufacturing space, Colson Europe and its affiliates employ 420 people.[49] Its 1999 acquisition of Castors International, based in West Midlands, England, increased Colson Europe's presence in the United Kingdom and abroad.[50]

Shepherd Caster, which joined The Marmon Group in 1990, has a 112,100-square-foot facility that employs 95 in St. Joseph, Michigan. The company owes its name to George Shepherd, an Australian engineer who developed and refined the 2.5-inch ball during the 1930s and 1940s. It was this invention that made Shepherd a household name in the furniture caster business. The company also manufactures and markets a complete line of metal and plastic ball and wheel casters for appliances, medical equipment, and store fixtures as well as for material-handling applications.[51]

### Industrias Metalicas Sudamericanas, S.A.

IMSA manufactures material-handling products and components, including casters and wheels, and store fixtures for Latin American markets. Based in Medellin, Colombia, the company also has facilities in Guayaquil, Ecuador, and Valencia, Venezuela. IMSA operates a total of 132,000 square feet of manufacturing and warehouse space and employs 195 people.[52] Founded in 1957, IMSA has been associated with The Marmon Group since 1961. In 1999, all still outstanding shares of the firm were acquired through a Marmon Group member company.[53]

A Colson caster. Colson has grown tremendously as a member of The Marmon Group, offering a line of 35,000 casters.

## Shepherd Products, Inc.

Shepherd Products manufactures ball-type, twin-wheel plastic casters for home furniture, office chairs, and appliances, as well as office chair bases and chair components, including arms, seat pans, chair backs, standpipes, and covers. Founded in 1957, the company became a Marmon Group member in 1990. Since then, Shepherd Products has grown substantially.

The company expanded its manufacturing base into the People's Republic of China and built a new, 50,000-square-foot facility in Guangzhou.[54] In 2000, the company built a modern, 130,000-square-foot manufacturing plant in Brampton, Ontario.[55] In addition to its manufacturing locations, Shepherd has a distribution center in Santa Fe. The company employs 315 people.

## Shepherd Hardware Products Ltd.

Instead of manufacturing and producing its own goods, Shepherd Hardware Products buys its consumer floor-care products (casters, leg tips, and self-adhesive floor protection pads) and other consumer hardware items for packaging and sale to major retailing companies located in North America, the United Kingdom, Europe, South America, and Australia.[56]

Based in Richmond Hill, Ontario, Shepherd Hardware Products was established soon after Shepherd Products joined The Marmon Group in 1990.

Today, the company and its affiliates have operations totaling 278,000 square feet and employing 185 people.

Chair base and caster from Shepherd Products and Shepherd Caster, respectively

The Marmon Group's water treatment companies include EcoWater, a maker of residential water purification systems.

CHAPTER EIGHT

# Medical & Water Products

## Medical Products

**Pearsalls Limited**
**MicroAire Surgical Instruments, Inc.**
**OsteoMed Corporation**
**Acumed, Inc.**
**American Medical Instruments, Inc.**
**Manan Medical Products, Inc.**
**Medical Device Technologies, Inc.**
**Surgical Specialties Corporation**
**B. G. Sulzle, Inc.**

## Water Treatment Systems

**Graver Technologies, Inc.**
**Spectrum Labs, Inc.**
**Alamo Water Refiners, Inc.**
**Ecodyne Limited**
**EcoWater Systems, Inc.**

## MEDICAL PRODUCTS

The Marmon Group's first experience with medical equipment came in the early 1950s with a division of the Colson Company; today the Group includes numerous medical products firms. Several of these have joined The Marmon Group since 1997, bringing total annual revenues in the medical businesses to more than $200 million.[1]

### Pearsalls Limited

Pearsalls, a British company that joined The Marmon Group in 1999,[2] has the distinction of being the oldest firm to have become a Marmon member. It can trace its beginnings back to 1795 as a silk wholesale and retail business.[3]

Pearsalls conducts business under three trading names: Pearsalls Sutures, Pearsalls Implants, and Pearsalls Surgical. Pearsalls Sutures makes approximately four hundred kinds of suture thread for surgeries ranging from ophthalmic to veterinary. Pearsalls Implants develops and manufactures textile implants to help repair torn muscles, arteries, and discs. Pearsalls Surgical supplies sterile surgical patties (neurological swabs) to many major U.K. hospitals and distributors worldwide.

At its 50,000-square-foot plant in Taunton, U.K., Pearsalls has 55 employees and fourteen hundred braiding machines that run twenty-four hours a day, seven days a week, including "lights out" manufacturing. Approximately 2 million meters of braided suture is produced each week. That's about 3 million individual sutures. Approximately 70 percent of the production is braided silk and 25 percent is braided polyester. Monofilament nylon and silk microsutures are also produced. Approximately 90 percent of Pearsalls' production is exported.

### MicroAire Surgical Instruments, Inc.

Based in Charlottesville, Virginia, MicroAire came into the Marmon fold in 1978 with the acquisition of American Safety Equipment. It has grown through other acquisitions, such as its 1994 purchase of Precision Edge Surgical Products, a Sault Ste. Marie, Michigan, manufacturer of burs and blades, and Northeast Surgical Tool. Today, MicroAire designs, develops, and produces both air-powered and electric-powered orthopedic surgical instruments, and also manufactures a full line of accessories for its own instruments as well as burs and blades for tools made by other manufacturers.

Left: MicroAire was one of the first medical products companies to join The Marmon Group. Among its products is this powered surgical instrument.

Opposite: MicroAire makes a variety of surgical instruments, both air- and electric-powered, including this bur. Below left is a MicroAire drill, and below right is a MicroAire saw. The company, based in Charlottesville, Virginia, sells its products through a network of 37 distributors in the United States and representatives in 53 other countries.

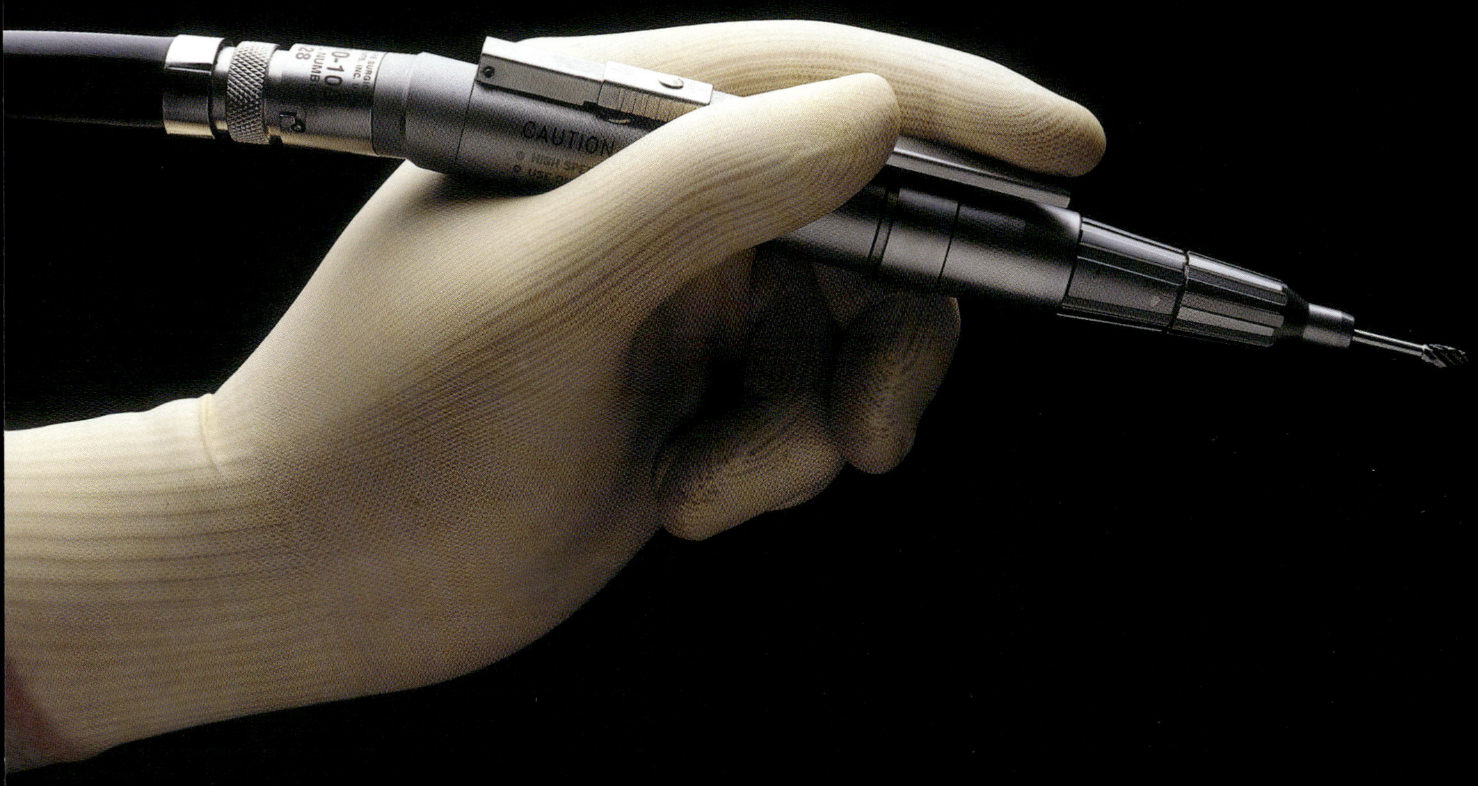

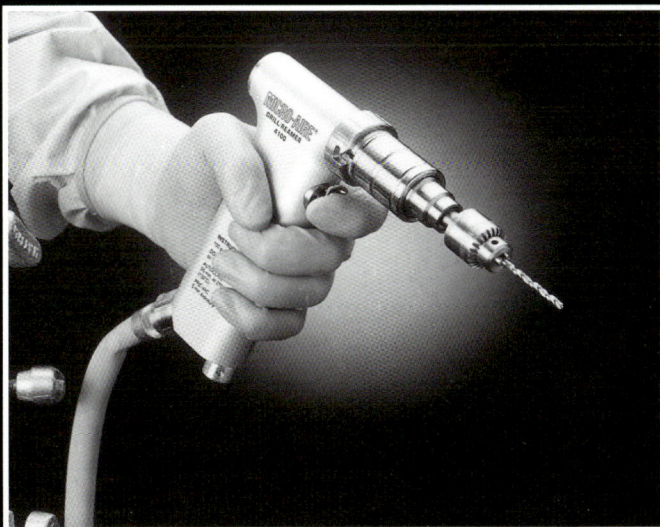
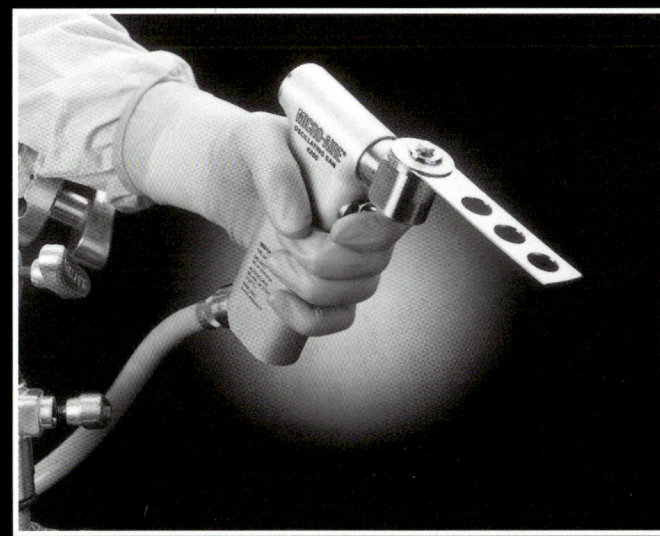

In 1999, MicroAire introduced two new products: an air-powered device for liposuction and an endoscopic carpal-tunnel treatment system. The firm has 37 U.S. distributors and is represented in 53 countries. With combined manufacturing space of about 100,000 square feet, MicroAire has 240 workers.[4]

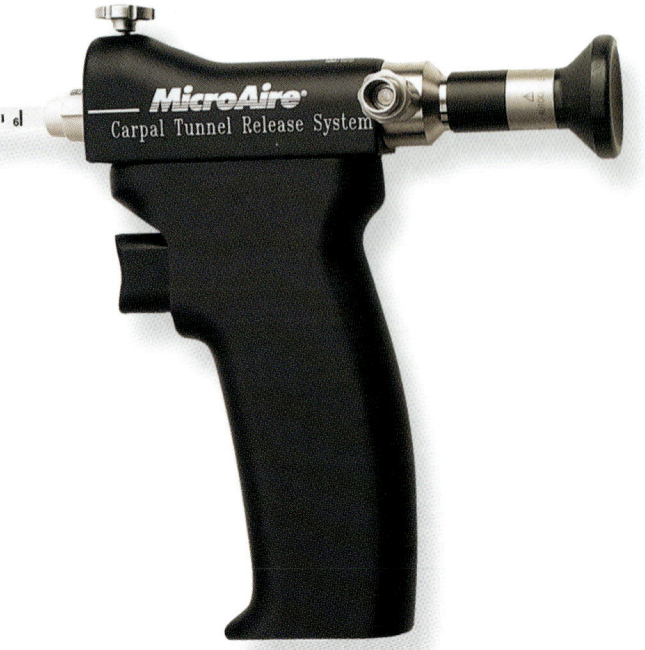

A MicroAire carpal tunnel release system, introduced in 1999 as an endoscopic treatment

### OsteoMed Corporation

OsteoMed, a Marmon Group member company since 1999, manufactures specialty medical devices and surgical implants used in oral-facial, neurological, and orthopedic surgery to help shape, cut, secure, reconstruct, and regenerate bone. The firm's principal products are fixation devices and systems which use specialized titanium screws or plates to fix small bone fractures, osteotomies, and bone grafts. Other products include a modular power-tool system, a bone-harvesting device used for bone grafting, a battery-powered surgical headlight, and a first metatarsal toe implant. In the United States, sales are handled by 38 direct sales representatives. Internationally, OsteoMed has 39 distributors in 32 countries. Headquartered in a 32,000-square-foot plant in Addison, Texas, the firm has 130 employees.[5]

### Acumed, Inc.

A Marmon Group member company since 1999, Acumed designs, manufactures, and markets orthopedic implants and instruments used in the surgical treatment of fractures in the upper extremities (fingertips to shoulder) as well as the foot and ankle. Its products are sold to hospitals and trauma centers worldwide—in the United States through a network of approximately 200 sales representatives and internationally through authorized distributors.

Based in Beaverton, Oregon, the firm has a 55,000-square-foot facility with 100 employees.[6]

### American Medical Instruments, Inc.

Founded in 1973, American Medical joined The Marmon Group in 1994. And even though its existing factory in Massachusetts was upgraded after the takeover, soon a new, 57,000-square-foot facility needed to be built in Dartmouth, Massachusetts, to handle the firm's growing business. The company produces and sells—primarily to other medical equipment manufacturers that distribute their finished products to hospitals and doctors worldwide—a wide range of needles used by physicians for a variety of procedures, including general anesthesia and chemotherapy. The company's needles are also used to remove tissue samples for biopsies of the lung, liver, pancreas, breast, and other soft tissues. American Medical also produces cannulas, small tubes inserted into body cavities to drain fluid or inject medications. The firm employs approximately 150 people.[7]

## Manan Medical Products, Inc.

Manan Medical, another manufacturer of specialty medical needle products, joined The Marmon Group in 1997. Based in Wheeling, Illinois, the firm's 82,000-square-foot facility is staffed by 140 employees and manufactures needle products for biopsy, oncology, mammography, cardiology, and anesthesia procedures. Manan also produces a patented spring-loaded automatic biopsy gun, used to take sample tissue in suspected cancer cases, that has become an industry standard.[8]

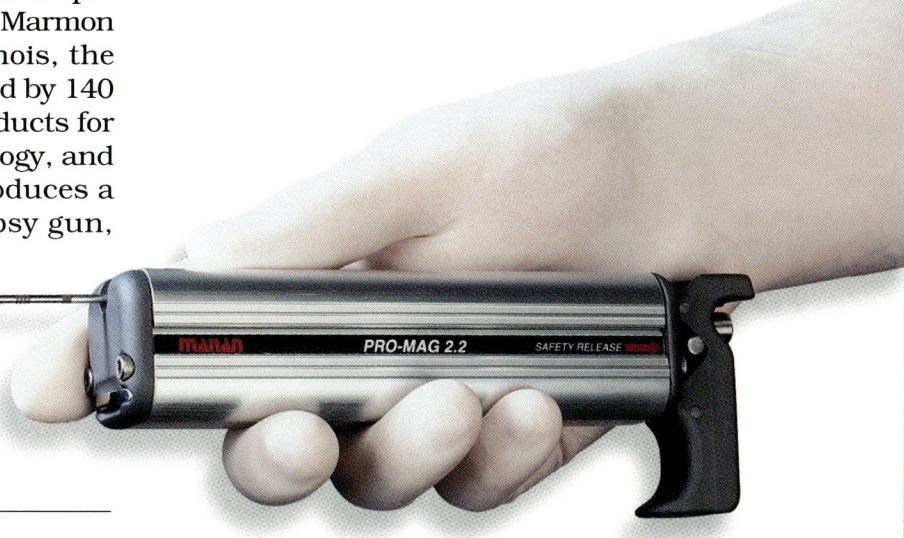

Manan Medical Products joined The Marmon Group in 1997. The company, based in Wheeling, Illinois, manufactures a wide variety of needle products as well as a patented biopsy tool.

## Medical Device Technologies, Inc.

Medical Device Technologies, founded in 1986 as National Standard Medical Products, joined The Marmon Group in 1990 and became the marketing and distribution arm for Manan Medical Products when that firm joined the Group in 1997.[9] Based in Gainesville, Florida, the company's 42,000-square-foot facility and its 125 employees produce and distribute breast lesion localization needles, automated biopsy instruments, and other biopsy needles used by physicians in minimally invasive human organ and bone biopsy procedures. The firm also supplies needles for isotope seeding of the prostate gland, catheters for drainage procedures, and specialty needles and guide wires used by doctors for catheter placement.

Medical Device Technologies markets its products throughout the United States, as well as in Germany, Japan, Canada, the United Kingdom, Italy, France, Spain, and Australia.[10] Medical Device Technologies further expanded into the international market in 1999 with the purchase of PBN Medicals Denmark A/S. Based

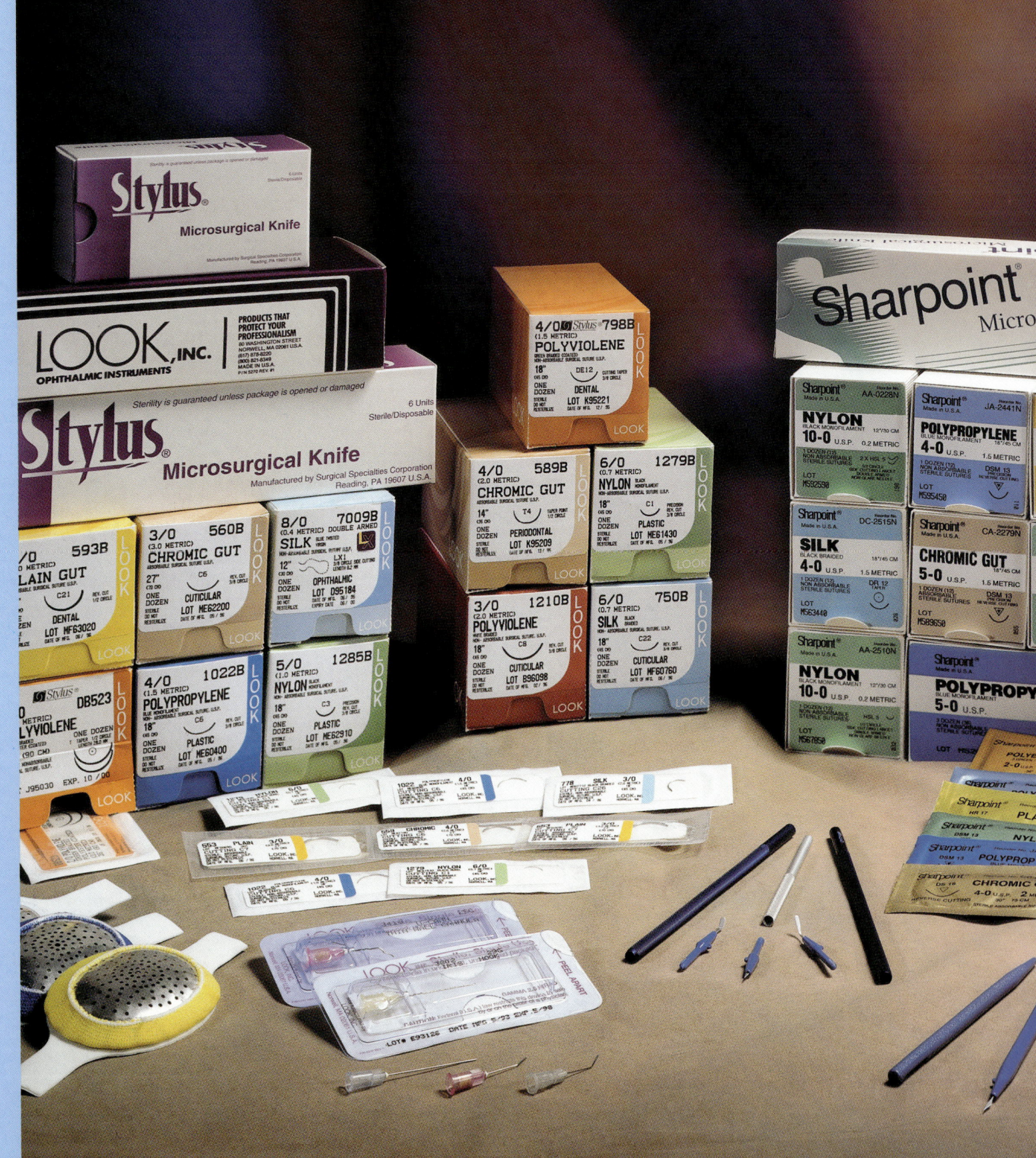

# CHAPTER EIGHT: MEDICAL & WATER PRODUCTS

in Stenlose, Denmark (near Copenhagen), PBN Medicals Denmark manufactures and sells a variety of single-use products, including such medical equipment as catheters, guide wires, needles, dilators, and stents.[11] The company employs 85 people at its 30,000-square-foot manufacturing facility.

## Surgical Specialties Corporation

Acquired in 1997, Exeter, Pennsylvania-based Surgical Specialties is a manufacturer and supplier of surgical needles, sutures, and knives used in ophthalmological, dental (oral and periodontal), cardiovascular, plastic, and reconstructive surgery, in addition to microsurgery and veterinary surgery. Its products are sold for private-label distribution by multinational companies in the surgical products industry, as well as under its own brand names. In addition to its plant and office in Pennsylvania, Surgical Specialties has a plant in Ada, Oklahoma, which specializes in the design and manufacture of precision products for difficult procedures.[12] In 1999, the firm expanded its presence in the dental suture market when it purchased the assets of Cottrell International of Englewood, Colorado.[13] Combined, Surgical Specialties has 158,400 square feet of manufacturing space and employs 450 people.[14]

## B. G. Sulzle, Inc.

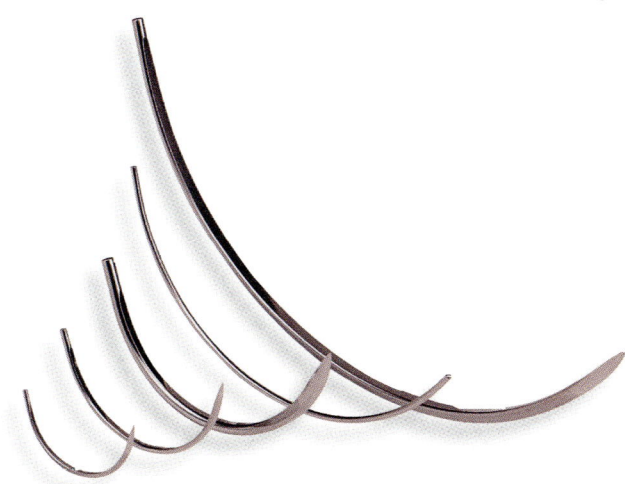

While B. G. Sulzle also manufactures surgical needles, they have very different applications from the ones produced by American Medical, which are essentially hollow instruments for introducing medication or removing materials from the body. The needles manufactured by B. G. Sulzle are designed primarily to carry sutures for sewing tissues in surgery. The firm produces more than twenty-five hundred varieties of such needles for suture manufacturers the world over. Its products are employed in a wide range of specialties, including dentistry, cardiology, gynecology, orthopedics, and plastic surgery.

The North Syracuse, New York, company got its start in 1945, when engineer and inventor Benjamin Sulzle set out to produce innovative, high-quality surgical needles. His love of design and innovation led him to invent the atraumatic drilled-end needle, which at the time marked a breakthrough in surgical needle design.[15] B. G. Sulzle's 80,000-square-foot plant has more than 300 employees.[16]

Above: A selection of surgical needles from B. G. Sulzle. Sulzle's products are designed to carry medical sutures and are used in a variety of medical specialties.

Above right: A surgical knife from Surgical Specialties. A maker of various needles, sutures, and knives, Surgical Specialties joined The Marmon Group in 1997.

Opposite: A line of needles and other medical products manufactured by Surgical Specialties, which became a Marmon Group member company in 1997.

EcoWater's products, including water conditioners and reverse osmosis systems, are sold through a network of 1,400 distributors and major retailers on six continents. The company is based in St. Paul, Minnesota, and has almost 700 employees.

# Water Treatment Systems

Marmon Group member companies provide a variety of products for the treatment of water in both residential and industrial settings. These companies operate worldwide.

### Graver Technologies, Inc.

Graver Technologies joined The Marmon Group in 1981 as a part of the Trans Union acquisition. Based in Glasgow, Delaware, the company manufactures products that specialize in the trace contaminant removal and purification of process water, liquid sugar, fluids, compressed air, and process gases. The firm has four divisions, based upon the filtration technologies employed: the Adsorbents Division, also based in Glasgow, manufactures high-efficiency organic and inorganic adsorbents and carbon-block cartridges; the Industrial Filter Division, based in Honeoye Falls, New York, designs and manufactures a complete line of air and gas filtration systems and replacement elements; the Ion Exchange Division, based in Newark, New Jersey, manufactures specialty ion exchange resins used to purify condensate water; the Liquid Filter Division, based in Glasgow, manufactures back-washable and disposable liquid filter cartridges and stainless steel filter membranes.

Graver Technologies entered the European market in 1998 with the purchase of Spezialfilterbau Walter Beck, a German producer of filter elements for the power generation, food and beverage, and wastewater treatment markets.

Combined, the company has 240,000 square feet of manufacturing space and 180 employees.

Right: An industrial filter from Graver Technologies. Graver joined The Marmon Group in 1981 as part of the Trans Union acquisition.

Above left: A Graver Technologies air filter. The company makes products to remove trace contaminants and purify process water, other fluids, and gases.

### Spectrum Labs, Inc.

Spectrum Labs provides water, soil, and hazardous-waste testing for both individual consumers and industry.

Spectrum also sells chemicals and soap products used within the water treatment and purification industry. Additionally, Spectrum Labs conducts product testing for manufacturers of water conditioning equipment. Located in St. Paul, Minnesota, the company's 24,000-square-foot facility has 20 employees.

### Alamo Water Refiners, Inc.

Alamo Water Refiners became a Marmon Group member in 2000. The company is a leading distributor of residential water treatment systems. It also designs and manufactures standard and customized water treatment products sold through dealers and private-label accounts in commercial, industrial, and institutional markets.

Alamo operates a 77,100-square-foot facility in San Antonio, Texas, and smaller plants in Odessa, Florida, and Greenville, Pennsylvania.

At another plant, in Barrington, Illinois, Alamo custom manufactures plastic components, including hubs, riser tubes, flanges, and brine valves, which are used in a wide variety of residential, commercial, institutional, and industrial water treatment systems worldwide. And in Naperville, Illinois, Alamo designs and manufactures commercial and industrial water treatment and purification systems. Alamo employs 140 people at facilities totaling 175,000 square feet.

### Ecodyne Limited

A member of The Marmon Group since the Trans Union acquisition in 1981, Ecodyne designs and manufactures industrial water treatment equipment and systems worldwide. It is headquartered near Toronto, Canada. Ecodyne's main markets include power generation plants, oil and gas refineries, chemical plants, and pulp and paper mills, as well as municipal water and wastewater treatment systems that eliminate organic and mineral particles and other contaminants from raw lake and river water, making it fit for human consumption. Although Canada is the firm's largest market, Ecodyne systems operate today in more than thirty countries around the world. The firm's 49,000-square-foot plant employs 80 workers.

An affiliated company, Graver Water Systems, Inc., designs, engineers, manufactures, retrofits, refurbishes, and upgrades water and wastewater treatment equipment for industrial plants and electrical utilities on a global basis. Based in Cranford, New Jersey, the company operates a 20,000-square-foot plant and employs 45 people.

An Ecodyne Limited water treatment system, left. Ecodyne products, below, are used in a variety of industries, including power, oil and gas, chemical, and pulp and paper, and in municipalities.

# CHAPTER EIGHT: MEDICAL & WATER PRODUCTS

## EcoWater Systems, Inc.

A member of The Marmon Group since the Trans Union acquisition in 1981, EcoWater Systems is the world's largest manufacturer of residential water treatment and purification equipment. EcoWater sells through 1,400 dealers worldwide, plumbing wholesalers, and private-label customers.

Based in St. Paul, Minnesota, and with facilities and affiliates in Mississippi, Canada, Germany, Belgium, England, and France, the firm has 690 employees and a total of 555,000 square feet of manufacturing and warehouse space.

EcoWater Systems got its start in 1925 when the firm's founder, Lynn G. Lindsay, obtained his first patent for a water conditioning system. The company grew steadily until 1959, when it was purchased by the Union Tank Car Company.

An EcoWater water conditioner. EcoWater, a Marmon Group member company since 1981, is the world's largest manufacturer of residential water treatment and purification equipment.

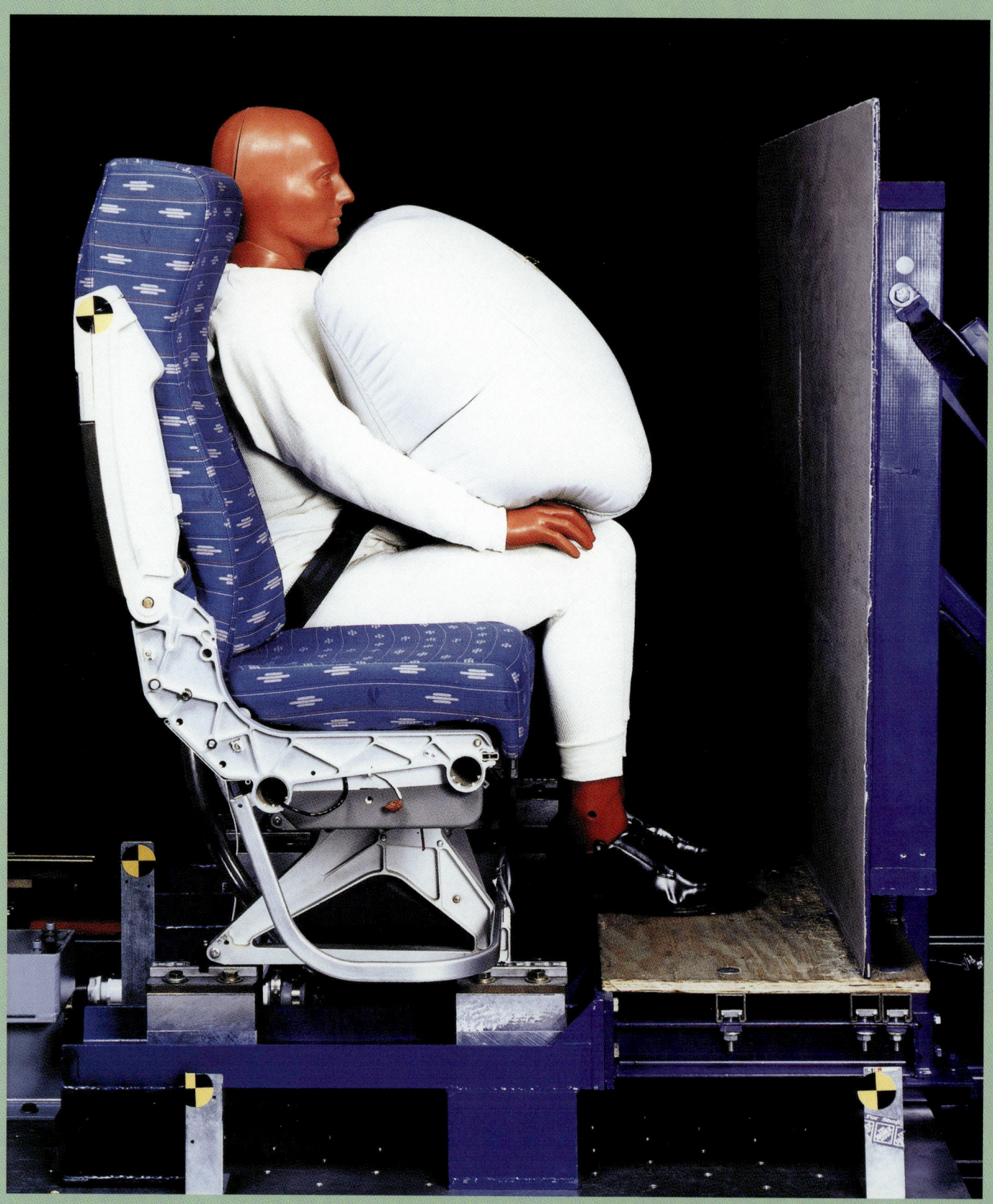

A test dummy demonstrates the safety of Am-Safe's inflatable seat belt. Besides passenger seat belts, Marmon Group member companies produce restraints for flight crews, cargo, and other uses.

CHAPTER NINE

# TRANSPORTATION

### HIGHWAY TRANSPORTATION EQUIPMENT

**Webb Wheel Products, Inc.**
**Detroit Steel Products Co., Inc.**
**Marmon-Herrington Company**
**Fontaine International, Inc.**
**Fontaine Modification Company**
**Fontaine Trailer Company**
**Perfection HY-Test Company**
**Triangle Suspension Systems, Inc.**

### SEAT BELTS AND CARGO RESTRAINTS

**Am-Safe Bridport Companies**

### RAIL AND TRANSPORTATION SERVICES

**Union Tank Car Company and Procor Limited**
**EXSIF Worldwide, Inc.**
**Penn Machine Company**
**Railserve, Inc.**
**Trackmobile, Inc.**
**IMPulse NC, Inc.**

## HIGHWAY TRANSPORTATION EQUIPMENT

The Marmon Group's automotive equipment companies represent some of the organization's earliest member companies. Webb Wheel Products has grown dramatically since it joined The Marmon Group, while the Triangle companies are leading spring and suspension manufacturers. Fontaine companies, meanwhile, service the heavy truck market.

### Webb Wheel Products, Inc.

Founded in 1946,[1] Webb Wheel Products joined Marmon in 1971 as part of the American Steel and Pump acquisition. At the time, this manufacturer of spoke wheels, hubs, brake drums, and rotors for the medium- and heavy-duty truck, trailer, and bus industries was a distant third among its competitors.[2] However, with new management, new products, increased marketing, and improved facilities, Webb Wheel Products has become one of Marmon's standout success stories and is widely recognized as the undisputed leader in its industry. As a Marmon member company, Webb Wheel Products' sales increased from $7.8 million when the firm was acquired in 1971 to more than $175 million in 2000.[3]

Left and opposite: Webb Wheel Products joined The Marmon Group in 1971 as a third-place competitor in its market. By 2001, it had become the leader in its industry.

As an indication of the Alabama-based company's growth, in 1998 the firm replaced its Siloam Springs, Arkansas, plant with a new, 293,000-square-foot manufacturing plant located on a 43-acre site in Siloam Springs.[4] In 1999, the firm's expansion continued with the purchase of a 69,000-square-foot manufacturing and warehousing facility, immediately expanded to 73,000 square feet—giving Webb a second plant in Cullman, Alabama. This expansion gave Webb Wheel the capacity to produce an additional 400,000-plus truck brake drums per year.[5]

The company has a total of 475 employees and 670,600 square feet of production space.[6]

### Detroit Steel Products Co., Inc.

Detroit Steel Products Co., Inc., a world leader in the design and manufacture of suspension products for trucks, trailers, buses, motor homes, and chassis manufacturers,[7] became affiliated with The Marmon Group in 1966 as part of the Fenestra deal.[8]

Founded in Detroit in 1904 by John G. Rumney—a one-time hardware salesman, Montana land and cattle speculator, and at the time, manager of a Kalamazoo, Michigan, firm that made flat-leaf springs for horse-drawn wagons—Detroit Steel is thought to be the first American firm organized specifically to manufacture automotive springs.[9]

Rumney moved to Detroit because it was becoming the nation's most important automotive center, hosting no fewer than twelve auto companies, including Ford, Cadillac, and Packard. Both the location and timing proved fortunate for the start-up firm as it began producing both automobile and railcar springs. Shortly after Rumney's small factory began production with a 20-man crew, one of the city's largest spring plants was destroyed by fire. As a result, his business boomed along with the auto industry. By 1922, Detroit Spring was providing 34 truck

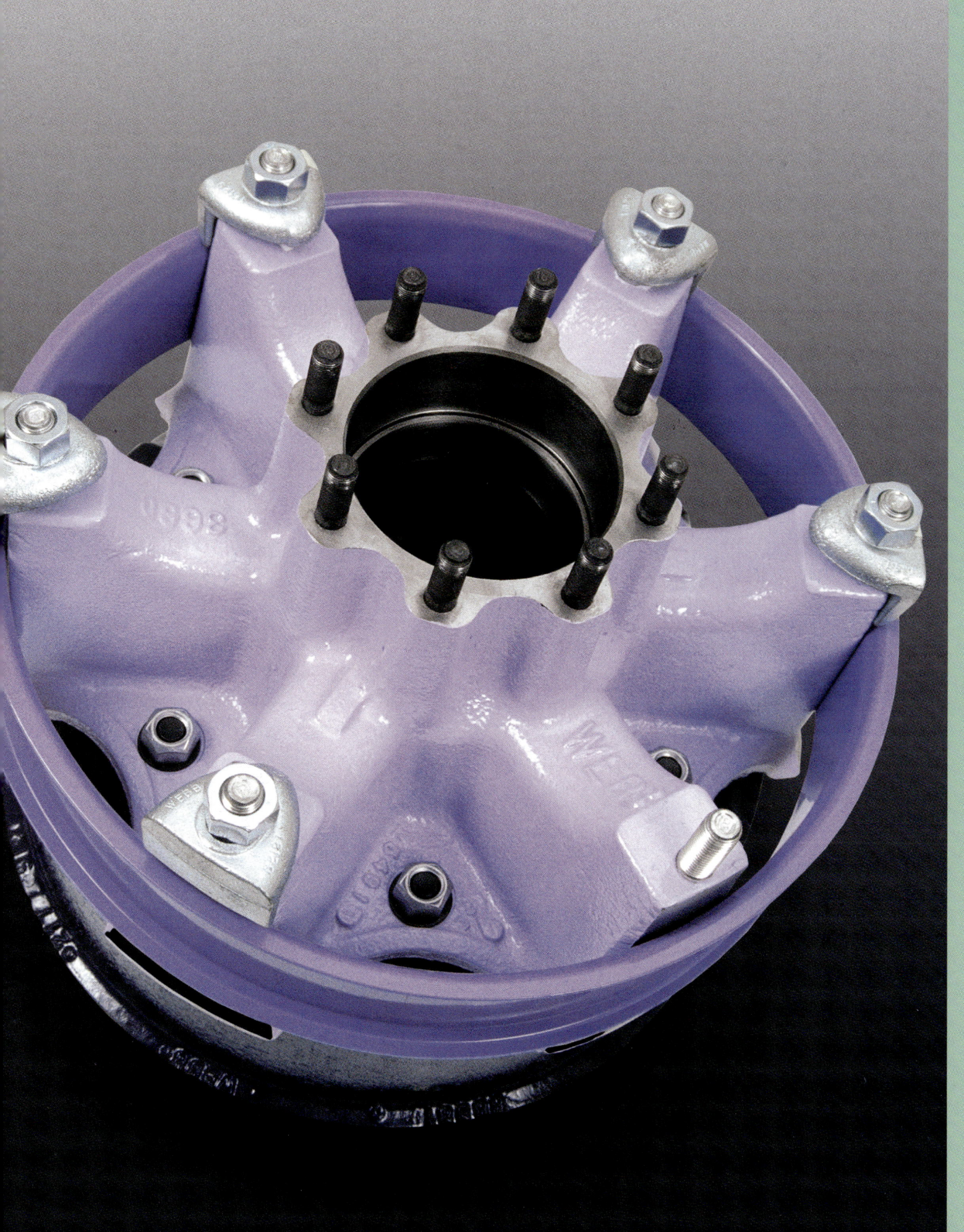

# MARMON
## PRESENTS A NEW CUSTOM SERIES

As a further step in its fine car program Marmon, collaborating with the finest custom builders, presents at the New York and Chicago salons and at leading Marmon establishments a new series of distinguished custom creations.

*Illustrated—Marmon Grand National—Sportsman's Convertible Sedan for five passengers. Marmon Big Eight chassis. Body by Locke.*

MARMON MOTOR CAR COMPANY, INDIANAPOLIS

# CHAPTER NINE: TRANSPORTATION

manufacturers and 24 passenger-car makers with its springs.[10]

The company remained in Detroit until 1979, when it moved its headquarters and all production to a much-expanded former satellite plant in Morristown, Indiana.[11]

The firm has 64,000 square feet of production space and employs approximately 25 people.[12]

Suspensiones DSP, S.A. de C.V. manufactures and distributes leaf springs to customers in Mexico and the United States. Suspensiones also distributes Flagg Suspension Parts and Triangle Air Spring products to Mexico's aftermarket. Based in Monterrey, Mexico, the company's facilities occupy 300,000 square feet and employ 370 people.[13]

## Marmon-Herrington Company

After its purchase by L. A. Darling in 1963, the Marmon-Herrington Company became the source of The Marmon Group's name.[14] Today based in Louisville, Kentucky, the firm produces pre-engineered kits used to convert standard-built trucks into four-wheel-drive vehicles. Its 33,000-square-foot plant employs 35 people.[15]

Historically, the first company that held the Marmon name was formed in 1851 as the Nordyke and Marmon Machine Company. It specialized in the manufacture of flour-mill machinery.[16]

Around the turn of the century, the firm entered the automotive field and was reborn as the Marmon Motor Car Company. It went on to produce luxury and performance cars for approximately thirty years. Noteworthy achievements include the Marmon Wasp, which won the first Indianapolis 500 race in 1911, and the Marmon Sixteen, one of the finest luxury touring sedans produced.[17]

With the Depression came a severe drop in the automobile market and another change in direction for the company. In 1931, Marmon's president, Walter C. Marmon, joined forces with Col. Arthur W. Herrington to form the Marmon-Herrington Company. Herrington, a former Harley-Davidson motorcycle test driver and engineer, became a developer and advocate of all-wheel-drive vehicles after watching them cut through the French mud while he was serving as an army truck driver during World War I.[18]

Despite the Great Depression, Marmon-Herrington prospered from the start. The company designed and produced rugged, all-terrain vehicles for military forces around the world, as well as for oil exploration companies located in the Middle East. They included the Iraqi Pipeline Company, for which Marmon-Herrington built what were then the largest trucks ever produced.[19]

During World War II, tens of thousands of all-wheel-drive vehicles, half-track trucks, and small tanks rolled off Marmon-Herrington's assembly line in a former Duesenberg automobile factory in Indianapolis.[20]

After the war, the company began to produce its main product line—kits for the conversion of conventional trucks into four-wheel-drive vehicles. In 1985, the firm moved to its present location in Kentucky.[21]

Both pages: Marmon Motor Cars (opposite) were known for their advanced engineering and classic style in the golden age of the American automobile. The company also made the Marmon Wasp, above, winner of the first Indianapolis 500 in 1911. Marmon-Herrington (logo, top), acquired in 1963, remained a leader in all-wheel-drive technology in 2001.

## Fontaine International, Inc.

Known as Fontaine Fifth Wheel Company when it joined The Marmon Group in 1984 as part of the Altamil Corporation merger,[22] Fontaine International manufactures heavy-duty tractor and trailer coupling devices.[23] These devices command a 33 percent market share in the United States and substantial market shares in Canada, England, and Mexico, as well as other countries.[24]

Given the company's market share, its customer list reads like a Who's Who of the trucking industry: Freightliner Corporation, Navistar International Transportation Corporation, Peterbilt Motors, Kenworth Truck Corporation, Mack Trucks, Inc., Volvo Trucks of North America, Ryder, Penske, Schneider National, J. B. Hunt Transport Services, Inc., Swift Transportation, and many others.[25]

Fontaine's growth in recent years has been achieved largely through strategic acquisitions. For example, Fleetline Products of Springfield, Tennessee, was purchased in 1999. In 2000, the British manufacturer VBG Limited, the U.K.'s largest manufacturer of truck and trailer-coupling devices, joined The Marmon Group. It has since changed its name to Fontaine International Europe, Ltd.[26]

Headquartered in Birmingham, Alabama, Fontaine International's facilities in the United States, Canada, Mexico, and the United Kingdom cover a total of 488,000 square feet and employ 235 people.[27] As Fontaine Fleetline Products, Inc., the company manufactures fenders, splash guards, tire carriers, and related truck parts. It employs 70 people at its 110,000-square-foot plant.

## Fontaine Modification Company

Also a part of the 1984 Altamil Corporation merger, Fontaine Modification Company operates facilities located near major truck manufacturers, where it converts, for both dealers and individual customers, standard-built trucks into all-wheel-drive, dual-drive, right-hand-drive, and stand-up-drive vehicles.

Other custom modifications include crew cab configurations and suspension and steering alterations. Based in Charlotte, North Carolina, Fontaine Modification has facilities in Louisville, Kentucky; Springfield, Ohio; and Dublin, Virginia. Together, they cover a total of 165,200 square feet and employ 155 people.[28]

## Fontaine Trailer Company

Fontaine Trailer Company also joined The Marmon Group in 1984 as a part of the Altamil Corporation merger. The firm manufactures a full line of platform trailers, including drop platform, low-bed, and other specialty trailers for heavy-duty hauling.[29]

The firm was founded in 1940 by John P. K. Fontaine as part of the Fontaine Truck Equipment Company in Birmingham, Alabama. It became a separate entity in 1964 when John Fontaine acquired the firm's current facility and headquarters, located in Haleyville, Alabama.

Since the firm joined The Marmon Group, it has prospered. The company's market share has grown from 3 percent to 25 percent, making Fontaine Trailer the leading platform-trailer company in the world.[30]

Acquisitions included the 1993 purchase of the Liddell-Birmingham Trailer Company, a designer and manufacturer of custom low-bed trailers and other specialty products. Renamed Fontaine Specialized, the product line is now a brand of Fontaine Trailer.[31]

In 1995, Fontaine Trailer formed a new division called Roadgear. The division is an aftermarket supplier of aluminum cab guards, aluminum and steel tool boxes, and replacement lights, as

---

Opposite: Fontaine Trailer joined The Marmon Group in 1984. The company manufactures a line of platform trailers, including drop platform, low-bed, and other specialty trailers for heavy-duty hauling.

well as other parts and accessories.[32] Roadgear also manufactures Mighty Lite Boat Docks, aluminum docks and gangways.[33]

Including its 1998 acquisition of a 300,000-square-foot manufacturing facility in Princeton, Kentucky, and its 2001 purchase of the assets of Ravens, Inc., a manufacturer of aluminum trailers with plants in Ohio, North Carolina, and Indiana, Fontaine Trailer has a total 1,080,200 square feet of manufacturing space and 670 employees.[34]

## Perfection HY-Test Company

Perfection HY-Test is a major supplier of new and remanufactured clutches for the automotive aftermarket.[35]

The current company was formed after several acquisitions were merged. The first company, Perfection American, resulted from the 1972 purchase of Active Gear Company, a Chicago-based manufacturer of replacement truck transmission gears.

In 1974, Perfection merged with the Darlington, South Carolina, gear division of Rexnord, a producer of manual transmission gears for cars and trucks.[36]

In 1980, Hy-Test Remanufacturers, a rebuilder and distributor of passenger car and light-truck clutches, water pumps, and other auto parts, joined The Marmon Group. It was merged with Perfection American under the Perfection HY-Test Company name. The new firm grew even larger with the 1989 purchase of a Florida-based remanufacturer of car and truck starter motors, alternators, and generators.[37]

Perfection HY-Test increased its reach in 1996 when it purchased a 78 percent interest in a firm that manufactures automotive parts in Xiapu, China.[38] The Chinese operation was renamed Ningbo Hongxie Machinery Manufacturing Co., Inc.[39]

Perfection employs 550 people at facilities totaling 308,000 square feet.

## Triangle Suspension Systems, Inc.

Since becoming a Marmon Group member in 1968,[40] the Triangle company, today a leading manufacturer of flat leaf springs, threaded rods, U-bolts, and other front-end parts for trucks and trailers, has expanded its product line by creating other companies.

Triangle, which was founded in Pittsburgh in 1919 and moved to its current headquarters in DuBois, Pennsylvania, eight years later, markets Triangle Air Springs, air springs for the auto, truck, and trailer aftermarket and the original equipment market, and Flagg Steel Products, components necessary to attach springs to vehicles.[41]

The company produces approximately 20,000 tons of product each year, which is marketed through a network of more than 700 distributors nationwide.[42] Triangle employs 240 people and

has a total of 330,000 square feet of production and warehouse space.[43]

Triangle Suspension Systems, Ltd., an affiliated company, manufactures and distributes a full line of leaf springs for the Canadian aftermarket. The company, headquartered in Cambridge, Ontario, has 150 employees and operates from a 138,000-square-foot plant.

Top: A Perfection HY-Test remanufactured clutch. Perfection HY-Test was formed by combining two members of The Marmon Group.

Above right: A leaf spring made by Triangle Suspension Systems. Triangle joined The Marmon Group in 1968 and is headquartered in DuBois, Pennsylvania. It employs 240 people.

# Seat Belts and Cargo Restraints

For many years, Am-Safe, Inc., has been the world's largest manufacturer of aircraft passenger safety belts. With the acquisition of the Bridport companies, based in the United Kingdom, Marmon Group member companies serve the entire cargo restraint industry, producing not only the restraints used to tie down cargo, but also the webbing from which straps are made.

### Am-Safe Bridport Companies

The Marmon Group entered the seat belt business in 1978 with the acquisition of American Safety Equipment Corporation. Today the Am-Safe Bridport Companies are the largest manufacturer of aircraft restraint systems and affiliated products in the world.

In 1987, Bob Pritzker sold nearly all of American Safety's seat belt and related manufacturing operations because of poor market conditions. He did, however, hold on to one small division of American Safety called Commercial Products, which specialized in the short-run production of passenger seat belts for commercial airlines and limited-run seat belt systems for trucks, farm equipment, and miscellaneous vehicles. Bob made the division a separate company and named it Am-Safe, Inc.[44] Today it is the largest manufacturer of aircraft passenger seat belts, flight attendant harnesses, pilot/copilot restraint systems, and inflatable restraints in the world. More than 500 commercial and business jet manufacturers use Am-Safe restraint products.[45] Based in Phoenix, Arizona, with additional facilities in Mesa, Arizona, as well as in China, the United Kingdom, and France, the firm's plants occupy 155,000 total square feet and employ approximately 300 people.[46]

Am-Safe Commercial Products, Inc., manufactures seat belt systems for off-road, recreational, and agricultural vehicles, as well as the truck/van conversion aftermarket. Based in Phoenix, Arizona, the company also has facilities in Mesa, Arizona; Elkhart, Indiana; and Surrey, England.[47]

Another element of the Am-Safe Bridport group is Am-Safe Textiles and Distribution. Composed of Brittanic Aviation, Londavia, Inc., Arthur Hart Webbing, Precision Weaving, and Avery Flight Interiors and Safetywear, these companies manufacture and distribute webbing and fabrics that are used in a wide variety of restraint systems.

Brittanic Aviation is a distributor for many of the world's leading manufacturers of aircraft equipment and consumable parts to airplane manufacturers, commercial airlines, maintenance facilities, and leasing and finance companies worldwide. Based in West Sussex, England, the firm's 6,000-square-foot facility is staffed by 10 employees.[48]

Londavia, Inc., based in Portsmouth, New Hampshire, joined The Marmon Group in spring 2001. An aircraft parts distributor, it complements Brittanic Aviation. It operates a 20,000-square-foot distribution facility.

Based in Somerset, England, Arthur Hart Webbing specializes in the manufacture of heavy and customized narrow fabric webbings in a variety of fibers for aerospace, defense, and industrial applications. With roots dating from 1789, Arthur Hart's current facility covers 65,000 square feet and employs 55 people. The company joined The Marmon Group in 1999 as part of the acquisition of Bridport PLC.[49]

Precision Weaving, a manufacturer of narrow fabrics, including seat belt webbing and finished cargo slings and straps, became a Marmon Group member in 1996 after Am-Safe purchased the assets of Technical Textiles and renamed the firm.

Am-Safe's headquarters, located in Phoenix, Arizona. The company employs about 300 people.

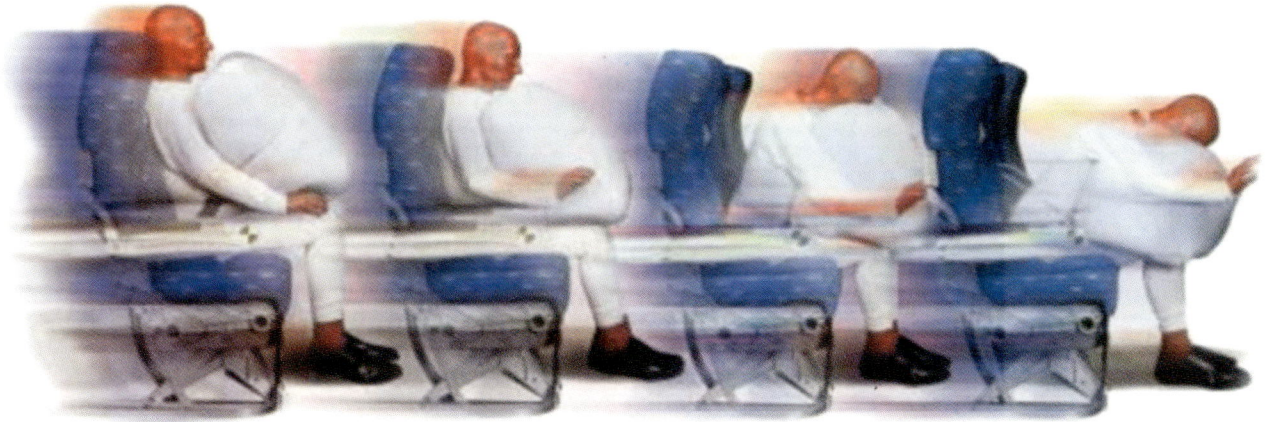

Based in Piedmont, South Carolina, Precision moved into a new, 78,000-square-foot facility in 2000.[50]

Also in the United Kingdom, Avery Flight Interiors and Safetywear supplies textile products and services to the commercial aviation sector. Its facility covers 18,000 square feet and employs 45 people.[51]

Finally, Bridport Aviation Products designs and manufactures a broad range of cargo restraint systems, including pallet nets and other equipment for major airlines. The company joined The Marmon Group in 1999 as part of the acquisition of Bridport PLC. Headquartered in Dorset, England, Bridport Aviation also operates plants in Middlesex, United Kingdom; Erie, Pennsylvania; Singapore; and Sri Lanka. The firm's facilities cover a total of 237,000 square feet and employ 250 people.[52]

A United States affiliate, Bridport Air Carrier, fabricates and supplies a full range of sewn products for the aerospace industry. Its products include air cargo restraints, as well as passenger safety items. Based in Kent, Washington, the firm's 20,000-square-foot plant has 45 employees.[53]

Militair Aviation supplies military aircraft spare parts, as well as repair and overhaul services, to air forces, navies, and maintenance organizations in more than forty countries. Headquartered in Hampshire, England, Militair also has facilities in Wake Forest, North Carolina, and Bathurst, Australia. Its facilities cover a total of 30,000 square feet and employ 33 people.[54]

Opposite and above: An inflatable seat belt produced by Am-Safe Bridport. This innovative seat belt was recently introduced.

Right: A cargo restraint produced by Am-Safe Bridport

## Rail and Transportation Services

Marmon Group member companies have a commanding position in the rail industry. Union Tank Car Company, with Canadian affiliate Procor Limited, is North America's leading lessor, manufacturer, and maintainer of railroad tank cars. EXSIF Worldwide, Inc., is the world's leading lessor of international tank containers. Marmon Group member companies IMPulse NC, Railserve, Penn Machine, and Trackmobile serve other parts of the rail industry, manufacturing and selling goods including wheels, electrification systems, and other products.

### Union Tank Car Company and Procor Limited

Union Tank Car Company, based in Chicago, and Procor Limited, based in Oakville, Ontario, both entered The Marmon Group in 1981 with the Trans Union merger. Combined, they are North America's leading manufacturer and lessor of railroad tank cars. Their 80,000 railcars are used primarily by the chemical, petroleum, and food industries in the United States, Canada, and Mexico. Major customers include Shell Oil, BP Amoco, Imperial Oil, Dow Chemical, and Celanese Chemicals.

Union Tank Car's U.S. fleet of more than 60,000 railcars includes hopper cars for the plastics industry. Its standard fleet of tank cars is used to ship a variety of cargos, including corn syrup, plastic pellets and resins, liquefied petroleum gas, various kinds of oils and acids, fertilizers, asphalt, sulfur—even tomato paste and beer.[55]

Union Tank Car has 1,207,300 square feet of manufacturing space at its plants in East Chicago, Indiana, and Sheldon, Texas. Its 12,000-ton hydraulic press in East Chicago, used to cold-form heavy steel sheets into tank heads, is the largest in the world.[56] The tank car company also has 1,493,800 square feet dedicated to repair and maintenance, including a repair network of 12 major shops, 35 mini shops, and 86 service vehicles. The firm employs approximately 2,000 people.[57]

Procor, founded in the 1930s,[58] leases stainless steel, carbon steel, and aluminum tank cars and specialty-freight railcars.[59] Its fleet of railcars exceeds 21,000 and is serviced by a repair facility network across Canada. The company employs about 600 people.[60]

The Union Tank Car Company dates to 1891, when it was incorporated by John D. Rockefeller. As Rockefeller spiraled upward in the oil industry, he expanded his domination of the national rail transportation system by taking over other railcar suppliers until his Standard Oil Trust owned most of the nation's tank cars.

When federal and state governments began flexing their new regulatory muscle against monopolies, Rockefeller's Union Tank fleet was an obvious target. On July 14, 1891, the Standard Trust dodged the assault by forming a separate corporation, the Union Tank Line.[61]

---

Opposite and above: Tank cars manufactured by Union Tank Car Company. With Procor Limited, Union Tank is North America's largest manufacturer and lessor of railroad tank cars. The companies joined The Marmon Group as part of the 1981 Trans Union merger. Union Tank Car was founded as part of John D. Rockefeller's Standard Oil Trust but peeled off in 1911, when the Trust was broken.

Though Union Tank Line was now technically independent, it was still owned by Standard Oil and served only the company's refineries. That configuration changed when the U.S. Supreme Court broke up the Standard Trust in 1911, and the Union Tank Line Company became truly independent. In 1919, the railcar manufacturer and supplier bolstered its finances by listing on the New York Stock Exchange. At that time, company executives changed its name to the Union Tank Car Company so investors wouldn't misperceive it as one of the railroads that had recently come under tight regulation.[62]

## EXSIF Worldwide, Inc.

When EXSIF Worldwide acquired the tank container leasing business of Transamerica Leasing in 2000, it created the world's largest fleet of intermodal tank containers. The acquisition complemented the 1999 purchase of tank lessor EXSIF SAS, a French company.[63]

EXSIF Worldwide's containers are suitable for global transportation, distribution, and storage of bulk liquids, chemicals, and gases. EXSIF Worldwide is based in Purchase, New York, and has a fleet of 25,500 container cars. The company has overseas operations in China, Australia, France, Germany, Japan, Singapore, and the United Kingdom. EXSIF Worldwide has 80 employees.

Right: An EXSIF intermodal tank container

## Penn Machine Company

Penn Machine is a leading supplier of wheel and axle sets for light-rail systems. It also manufactures and rebuilds gear sets for transit and industrial applications. In addition, the company manufactures replacement parts, gearing, and components for underground mining equipment, as well as gear products for locomotives and steel producers. Headquartered in Johnstown, Pennsylvania, its manufacturing facilities in Pennsylvania, Ohio, and Virginia total 253,000 square feet and 170 employees.[64]

Left: A gear and pinion from Penn Machine Company

## Railserve, Inc.

To help insulate itself from the cyclical sales common to specialized producers of capital equipment, in 1988 Trackmobile established Railserve,[65] a company that has grown to become the largest provider of in-plant rail services in North America. Itself a buyer and user of Trackmobile products, the firm offers industrial switching of railcars, loading and unloading services, locomotive leasing, car inspection, and track repair. Railserve, headquartered in Atlanta, Georgia, operates in more than 50 locations and has approximately 550 employees.[66]

Affiliated with Railserve is WCTU (White City Terminal and Utility)[67] Railway, a short-line railroad operating in White City, Oregon.[68] WCTU has 13 miles of track with access to approximately 30 industrial plants.[69]

## Trackmobile, Inc.

Georgia-based Trackmobile is the originator and nation's largest manufacturer of road-and-rail industrial railcar movers. The vehicles were introduced in 1950 as a relatively small, mobile alternative to more costly rail-bound locomotives. The company was acquired in 1987 by then–Marmon Group member Marmon Transmotive, which produced a similar railcar mover called the Switchmaster.[70] The two product lines were merged and are now produced at Trackmobile's 81,000-square-foot LaGrange, Georgia, plant, which has approximately 75 employees.[71]

A Trackmobile runs on rubber-tired wheels from one trackyard location to another, converts hydraulically to steel-wheel rail operation, and then couples to a freight car, borrowing its weight to gain the tractive power of a much larger track-bound conventional switching locomotive.[72] Prior to the Trackmobile's invention, companies moved railcars around in their plants or rail yards primarily with conventional locomotives, which frequently became trapped between railcars.[73] More than eight thousand Trackmobiles are in operation worldwide.[74]

A mobile railcar-moving vehicle produced by Trackmobile. Based in Georgia, Trackmobile is the nation's largest manufacturer of road and rail industrial railcar movers. The company joined The Marmon Group in 1987.

## IMPulse NC, Inc.

A member of The Marmon Group since 1995, IMPulse designs, manufactures, and installs electrical power equipment for mass transit systems, including substations and overhead electrification hardware for streetcar, electric trolley, commuter light rail, and heavy rail applications. For example, in 1997 IMPulse was awarded a $5 million contract to design, build, and test 15 self-contained integrated traction-power substations to supply electric power to Salt Lake City's Light Rail System in time for the 2002 Winter Olympics.[75]

Based in Mount Olive, North Carolina, IMPulse was founded in 1990 by a group of traction-power professionals, technicians, and craftspeople. This group had experience working together at the transit switchgear division of the Ohio Brass Company.[76]

Through internal investment and acquisition, IMPulse continues to maintain its leadership role in the traction-power industry. In 2000, the company announced three acquisitions: the EMC operating unit of the Ansaldo Company in Italy; the overhead transit line of Westinghouse Air Brake Technologies, and the transit rectifier business of ABB Automation.[77]

IMPulse's manufacturing facilities cover a total of 253,500 square feet and employ approximately 260 people.

A selection of wire and cable products made by some of The Marmon Group's member companies

CHAPTER TEN

# METALS

## WIRE AND CABLE PRODUCTS

Cerro Wire & Cable Co., Inc.
Cable USA, Inc.
General Cable Industries, Ltd.
Getty Connections, Ltd.
Harbour Industries, Inc.
Rockbestos-Surprenant Cable Corp.
Hendrix Wire & Cable, Inc.
Comtran Corporation
Owl Wire and Cable, Inc.
The Kerite Company

## METAL PRODUCTS AND MATERIALS

Penn Aluminum International, Inc.
Cerro Copper Products Co.
Cerro Metal Products Company
Anderson Copper and Brass Company

## WIRE AND CABLE PRODUCTS

Marmon Group member companies manufacture an array of electrical and electronic wire and cable for a wide variety of industries. Over the last five years, this business segment has experienced significant growth. Products from member companies can be found in the construction industry, the automotive business, and in electronics, among other sectors.

### Cerro Wire & Cable Co., Inc.

Cerro Wire & Cable became a Marmon Group member during the merger of the Cerro Corporation in 1976.[1] The firm is a leading manufacturer of a full line of wire and cable products used in the construction of residential, commercial, and industrial buildings, as well as for industrial electrical applications up to 35,000 volts.[2]

The company got its start in New York in 1891 as a small electrical supply shop on Manhattan's Lower East Side. Even though Edison's lightbulb had been in use for only years, the age of electricity had arrived, and the shop prospered. Then as now, copper was the preferred conductor due to its relatively low cost, high electrical conductivity, easy maleability, and resistance to wear and fatigue.[3]

Cerro products are marketed and sold through the Cerrowire, Circle Wire, Cerrocord, and Aetna Insulated Wire divisions. Cerrowire/Circle Wire markets copper and aluminum building wire, aluminum URD, and overhead conductor and submersible pump cable. Under the Cerrocord product line, Cerro also sells thermostat cable, fire and security alarm cable, sprinkler cable, landscape wire, lamp cord, coaxial cable, telephone cable, and temporary lighting. The Aetna division's products include 5kV to 35kV medium-voltage cable, 600-volt and medium-voltage armor cable, 600-volt building wire, and single- and multiconductor cable. Cerro products are sold to wholesale electrical distributors and OEMs as well as to the retail hardware market. The company maintains 16 warehouses, including manufacturing and distribution facilities in Hartselle, Alabama; Ogden, Utah; Crothersville, Indiana; and Virginia Beach, Virginia, for a total of 1.1 million square feet, and employs 730 people.[4]

Above left, below, and opposite: Cerro Wire & Cable, acquired in the 1976 Cerro Corporation merger, grew into The Marmon Group's largest wire and cable company. More than one hundred years old, Cerro manufactures and sells wire products through a variety of subsidiaries. Its wide range of products includes copper and building wire, pump cable, coaxial cable, telephone cable, medium- and high-voltage wire products, and many more. They are sold to commercial, retail, and OEM markets.

## Cable USA, Inc.

Cable USA was acquired by The Marmon Group in 1997.[5] The company designs and manufactures specialty high-temperature wire and cable used in a broad range of industrial applications, including transit, industrial power and instrumentation, and household appliances, as well as aerospace.

The company's Unitherm Division designs and manufactures an extensive line of thermally insulated tubing, temperature-controlled tubing, flexible heated hose products, and self-regulating heating cables used in industrial and commercial applications where precise control of fluids is required. Cable USA's Dekoron Division specializes in signal transmission products, such as multi-pair, control, and thermocouple extension cable.[6]

Founded in 1984, Cable USA has 165,000 total square feet of manufacturing space at its facilities in Naples (its headquarters) and Cape Coral, Florida, and Houston and Mt. Pleasant, Texas. The firm has 195 employees.[7]

## General Cable Industries, Ltd.

General Cable Industries, a British manufacturer of wire and cable products, also joined The Marmon Group in 1997.[8] Founded just six years earlier, in 1991, the company entered the cable business primarily for the production of high-quality copper cables used for telephone and alarm applications. Today, General Cable Industries designs and manufactures a wide variety of wire and cable products, including category-five cable, used to network computers; fixed-wire cable, used for industrial power and lighting; and internal coaxial cable, used for voice and data transmissions.[9] The firm markets its products to more than 30 different countries, primarily in Europe and throughout the Middle East region.

Based in Thatcham, England, the company's 75,000-square-foot facility employs 70 people.[10]

## Getty Connections, Ltd.

Since its founding in 1986, Getty Connections has evolved into one of the world's leading manufacturers of cable and interconnection equipment for the telecommunications, electronics, and power supply industries.[11] It became a member of The Marmon Group in 1999.[12]

Based in Northern Ireland, Getty manufactures cable, cable assemblies, and general equipment wire for the telecommunications, electronics, power supply, automotive, and other industries. The firm offers full production, from initial extrusion, insulation, and sheathing of raw copper wire and tinsel into cabled wire, to the final assembly of a wide range of telephone cord sets, electronic lead assemblies, automotive harnesses, cable assemblies used with mobile telephone accessories, patch cords, and molded cable assemblies.[13]

Getty customers include such notable telecommunications manufacturers as Ericsson, Nortel, ST Microelectronics, and Elektromekan. Exports to more than 20 countries account for approximately 80 percent of Getty's sales.[14]

In 1998 the firm was named Northern Ireland Exporter of the Year, and in 1999 Getty Connections received the Queen's Award for Export Achievement, one of the United Kingdom's most prestigious industrial awards.[15]

In addition to its Northern Ireland headquarters in Belfast, Getty operates two plants in England, at Bishop Auckland and Skegness. The firm also

---

Opposite: A display of products from Getty Connections, which joined The Marmon Group in 1999. Getty is based in Northern Ireland and manufactures cable and connectors for telecommunications, electronics, and the automotive and other industries.

has a presence in China through Dongguan Getty Electronics Products Company, based in Dongguan City. Combined, the firm's facilities cover 145,500 square feet and employ 330 people.[16]

## Harbour Industries, Inc.

Harbour Industries manufactures a wide variety of high-performance wire and cable products. Based in Shelburne, Vermont, the company joined The Marmon Group in 1994. With its facility in Quebec, Canada, Harbour has a total of 135,000 square feet of production space and employs 190 people.[17]

The firm produces its goods for four specialized markets. Harbour's industrial wire and cables, made of material capable of withstanding heat, abrasion, and direct flame contact, are available for power supply use in consumer appliances and industrial food-service equipment, as well as in consumer electronics.[18]

Harbour's Premise Networking cables are used in local area computer networks, cable television systems, security systems, and other building system controls.[19]

Harbour entered the fast-growing communications cable arena in the early 1990s with products used in cellular telephone base stations and microwave communication base stations, which in turn are used in telecommunications, television, and radar systems.

The company also continues to serve its original market as a wire and cable supplier to military and commercial aircraft manufacturers. Its PTFE insulated lead wire is used in several applications, including radar systems, wiring systems used to launch missiles, and data-gathering devices, known as black boxes, carried on commercial aircraft. Harbour Industries also supplies coaxial cables used in the collision avoidance antenna systems now required in the cockpit of all commercial aircraft in the United States.[20]

## Rockbestos-Surprenant Cable Corp.

The Rockbestos Company became a part of The Marmon Group in 1976 during the Cerro Corporation merger.[21] Through a series of acquisitions that occurred during the next twenty years, the firm grew to become a leader in the design and manufacture of insulated high-performance, control, power, instrumentation, and specialty electrical cables.[22]

In 1996, Rockbestos doubled in size by acquiring the Surprenant Cable Corporation. Indeed, the deal created the largest specialized low-voltage cable manufacturer in North America.[23]

The firm's most recent acquisition occurred in 1999, when Rockbestos-Surprenant purchased the assets of the PMC Corporation, a manufacturer of engineered wire and cable products used within the temperature-sensor industry.[24]

Headquartered in Clinton, Massachusetts, Rockbestos-Surprenant makes products for applications in which exposure to high temperatures, radiation, moisture, corrosive atmospheres, or other harsh environmental hazards are expected.[25] Rockbestos-Surprenant cable products are used in applications as diverse as subway cars, nuclear utilities, and jet engines.[26]

Including its facilities in East Granby, Connecticut, and Manchester, New Hampshire, the company has 715,100 total square feet of manufacturing space and 500 employees.[27]

## Hendrix Wire & Cable, Inc.

Hendrix Wire & Cable, a manufacturer of electrical distribution cable, cable systems, and accessories for both aerial and underground utility applications, joined The Marmon Group in 1996. Based in Milford, New Hampshire, the company operates a 250,000-square-foot facility that employs 175 people.[28]

The firm was founded in 1951 by Bill Hendrix. His goal was to manufacture and market an overhead electrical distribution system that could withstand typically harsh New England winters and require little space. His creation—covered conductor wire suspended from a sturdy "messenger" wire—was called Spacer Cable and solved the reliability and limited-space problems that local utilities were experiencing. Spacer Cable eliminated power outages caused by harsh elements in the environment. Other benefits were soon recognized, including less tree trimming, fewer right-of-way concerns, ease of operation in contaminated environments, and the ability to span long distances, such as wide rivers and major highways.[29]

Employees at Hendrix Wire & Cable inspect cable. Hendrix was founded with the goal of introducing an overhead cable system that could withstand the harsh winters of New England. Its products are sold throughout the United States.

## Comtran Corporation

In 2001, Comtran Corporation joined The Marmon Group. Based in Whitinsville, Massachusetts, Comtran manufactures electronic, telecommunications, and fire alarm cable for customers throughout North America. It was founded in 1985 and operates from a 185,000-square-foot manufacturing facility. With 115 employees, Comtran sells its products through a national network of manufacturer representatives and distributors.

## Owl Wire and Cable, Inc.

Founded in 1954 to help meet the growing consumer demand for major electrical appliances, Owl Wire and Cable became a Marmon Group member in 1999.[30] Today the company manufacturers uninsulated copper wire for the automotive, building wire, appliance, and telecommunications industries. The firm's 210 employees, working in a 205,000-square-foot facility in Canastota, New York, produce more than 5 million pounds of copper product each week.[31]

Owl Wire and Cable's acquisition by The Marmon Group also included its sister corporation, Raven Wire & Cable, and a third firm, Owl Wire Logistics. Raven Wire manufactures a complementary product line of fine wire for electronics and other applications at a facility in Carrollton, Georgia, and serves customers in the southeastern United States, Texas, and Central America.[32] Raven's 58,000-square-foot plant employs 70 people.[33]

Owl Wire Logistics, a commercial contract carrier also based in Canastota, operates a fleet of tractor trailers and flatbeds used in the transportation of copper wire products.[34] Founded in 1989, Owl Wire Logistics has 65 employees.[35]

## The Kerite Company

The Kerite Company, a Marmon Group member since 1999, manufactures rubber-insulated power cable—capable of carrying from 600 to 138,000 volts—including underground distribution cable and power cable for use under water. The firm also provides a variety of other specialty cables and services. The company's 500,000-square-foot facility in Seymour, Connecticut, employs 160 people.[36]

The Kerite Company was founded in 1854 by Austin Goodyear Day, a nephew of the famous Charles Goodyear. Goodyear was the inventor who accidentally dropped some rubber mixed with sulfur on a hot stove, a process later known as vulcanization. This fortunate accident had the effect of strengthening the material so it could be applied to a vast variety of industrial uses, including automobile tires.[37] Before Goodyear's discovery, rubber products melted in hot weather, froze and cracked in cold, and adhered to virtually everything, which in turn greatly limited their usefulness. It was Charles Goodyear's invention that allowed his nephew's firm to subsequently achieve such milestones as insulated telegraph wire in 1865 and providing the underwater cables used in the 1908 construction of the Panama Canal.[38]

---

Opposite: Owl Wire and Cable was founded in 1954 to service the burgeoning post–World War II demand for cable used in home appliances.

Above: Rubber-insulated power cable produced by The Kerite Company. Kerite, which was founded in 1854, joined The Marmon Group in 1999.

## Metal Products and Materials

Penn Aluminum International, Cerro Copper Products, Cerro Metal Products, and Anderson Copper and Brass all joined The Marmon Group in the 1970s. These companies manufacture a wide variety of metal products that are sold to automotive, appliance, manufacturing, and many other markets.

### Penn Aluminum International, Inc.

Previously called Penn Brass & Copper, this Erie, Pennsylvania, firm was founded in 1923 and joined The Marmon Group in 1971. At that time, with the appliance and automotive industries using ever increasing amounts of aluminum instead of copper, Bob Pritzker thought the future was bright for aluminum.

Only a few months after the acquisition of Penn Aluminum International, copper tube production was halted, and experienced metallurgical and mechanical engineers were hired to develop more aluminum tube sizes and alloys. In 1977, the firm officially changed its name to Penn Aluminum International.[39]

In 1982, Penn replaced its old Erie facility by purchasing the Murphysboro, Illinois, plant of Indal, a Canadian conglomerate. Its modern, 38-acre, 190,000-square-foot aluminum extrusion plant produced rigid conduit and shapes for construction and transportation applications.[40]

This plant was then expanded to 220,000 square feet, an additional extrusion press was acquired, and new, high-speed drawing and coiling equipment was purchased to help produce aluminum tube to exact specifications for such applications as automotive air conditioning and consumer products.[41] Today Penn's Murphysboro facility covers 260,000 square feet and has 290 employees.[42]

### Cerro Copper Products Co.

When Cerro Copper Products joined The Marmon Group in 1976, it brought a long, eventful history of its own.

It was founded as the L. J. Cohen Company in 1908. Cohen was a dealer in scrap iron and other metals. He stayed in this trade for ten years, first in Kansas City and then in St. Louis. In 1918, however, Cohen died in an auto accident, and both the company's name and its direction changed.

Cohen's partner, William Lewin, renamed the enterprise Lewin Metals and brought his brother Tannie Lewin into the firm. Tannie thought more money could be made by recycling than by dealing in untreated metal, and soon the company began smelting brass ingot. At that time, copper reclamation consisted of smelting metal used in brass and bronze ingot. Higher-grade copper was refined from ore and was produced almost exclusively by major copper-mining companies. Tannie reasoned that a molecule of copper was a molecule of copper, regardless of origin. Consequently, if scrap copper could be refined, it would have the same properties as copper derived from ore.

The company began experimenting with electrolysis, the refining process used to make purer grades of copper. In the early 1920s, Lewin Metals built a pilot test plant, and by the mid-1920s secured a patent for the process. In 1927 the firm built a full-scale electrolytic refinery in Sauget, Illinois.

In 1931, the brothers merged with G. Mathes, another metals dealer, and the new firm was renamed the Lewin-Mathes Company. In 1939, it built its first copper tube mill. The objective was to produce copper plumbing tube that could compete with iron pipe. By the late 1930s, the easier-to-work-with and corrosion-resistant copper tube had largely replaced iron for both residential and commercial plumbing applications.

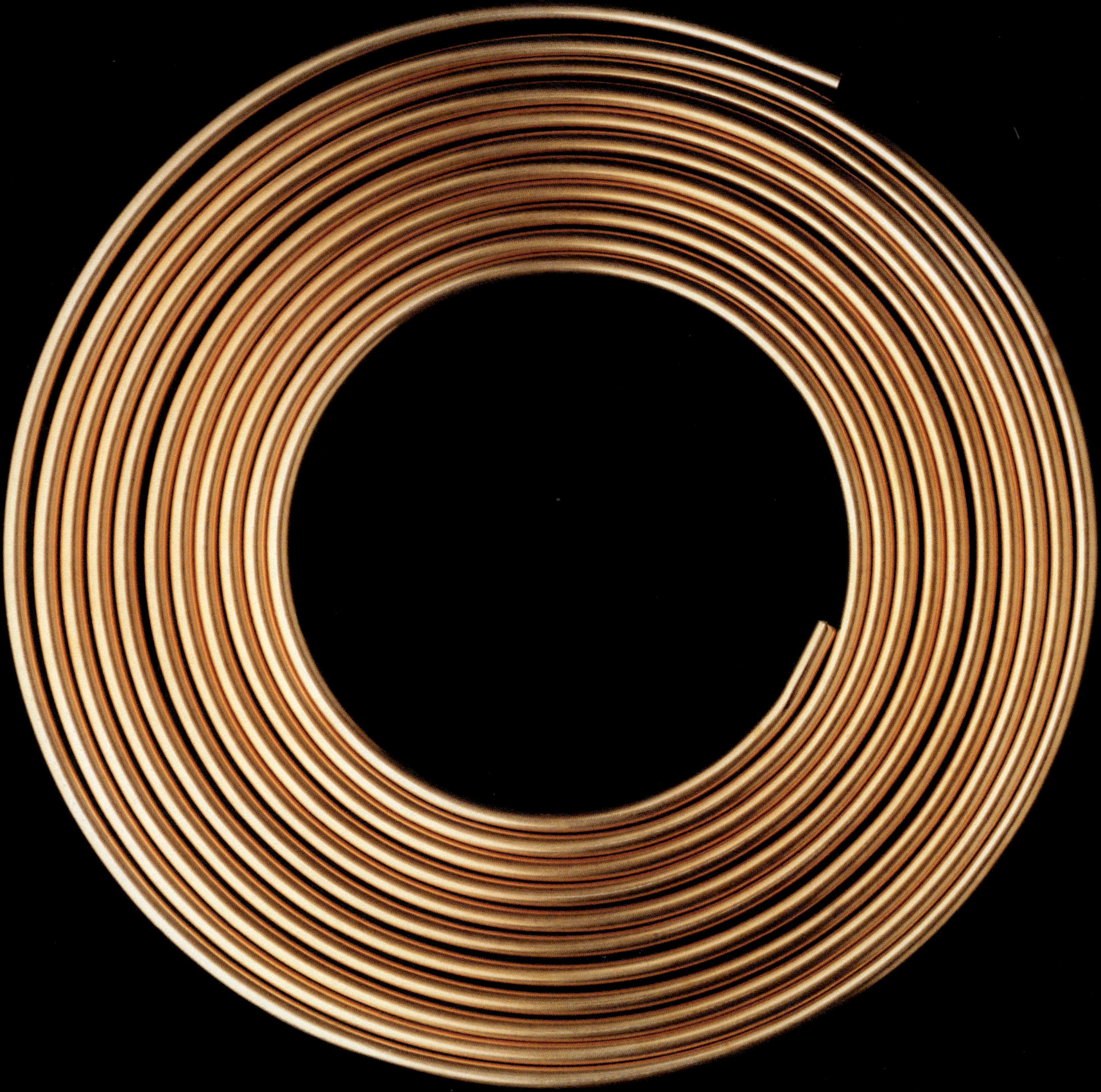

Cerro Copper Products joined The Marmon Group in 1976 during the Cerro Corporation merger.
It has grown into one of the world's largest manufacturers of copper tube.

During World War II, the company made parts for projectiles and tubing for combat and cargo ships. Wartime output tripled, and virtually all profits were reinvested to improve and enlarge Lewin-Mathes's facilities. After the war, the firm faced the biggest housing boom in United States history. Copper plumbing tube went into virtually every new home built. The replacement of iceboxes with refrigerators and the growing use of air conditioners over fans added to the demands on the company's tube mill.

In 1957, Lewin-Mathes became part of Cerro de Pasco, which financed construction of the present mill. In 1962, a state-of-the-art extrusion press was commissioned to begin a new era in copper tube production. Since becoming part of The Marmon Group, Cerro has continued to improve its systems and facilities. In 1981, the Shelbina, Missouri, plant began production of precision, thin-wall copper tube for industry. Now an affiliate of Cerro Copper Products called Cerro Copper Tube, it's one of the world's largest manufacturers of precision, thin-wall copper tube. Four manufacturing facilities (Shelbina, Missouri; Bossier City, Louisiana; Mexico, Missouri; and Sauget, Illinois) give Cerro three complete casting facilities and three extrusion presses capable of producing more than 300 million pounds per year. In June 2000, ground was broken for a new Cerro Copper Western Mill and Master Distribution Center in Cedar City, Utah, and limited operations began in fall 2001.[43]

Cerro Copper's facilities total 1,794,000 square feet and employ 1,130 people.

## Cerro Metal Products Company

Cerro Metal Products was one of several operating companies to join The Marmon Group in 1976 during the Cerro Corporation merger. Based in Bellefonte, Pennsylvania, since its founding in 1915 as Titan Metal Products, Cerro Metal manufactures brass rod, wire, forgings, and low-melt alloys as well as custom-machined forgings and automatic screw machine parts for the construction, decorative, and valve industries.[44] In 1999, Cerro maintained facilities in Paramount, California, and Weyers Cave and Shenandoah, Virginia, which covered more than 1 million total square feet and employed more than 1,000 people.[45]

Those totals went up in 2000 after Cerro's latest acquisition—the Accurate Forging Corporation. Based in Bristol, Connecticut, the business produces nonferrous aluminum and brass forgings at a 76,000-square-foot plant in Bristol and a 72,000-square-foot facility in Brave, Pennsylvania. The purchase also included a 13,000-square-foot metal grinding operation in West Hartford, Connecticut.[46]

To increase both its product lines and its global penetration, in 1999 four metalworking companies based in England were acquired to work in conjunction with Cerro Metals:[47]

• Cerro Precision Limited, in Brimsdown, manufactures custom-machined parts from brass, steel, aluminum, copper, stainless steel, and bronze. The firm also makes and distributes a line of industrial fasteners. Its 90,000-square-foot facility employs 150.[48]

• Cerro E.M.S. Limited produces nonferrous forgings, both as forged and machined, using conventional as well as fully automated equipment. Its factory in Walsall occupies 283,000 square feet and has 340 employees.[49]

• Cerro Extruded Metals Limited manufactures brass stamping rod, machining rod, hollow rod, profiles, and wire. The firm operates a 600,000-square-foot facility in West Bromwich and employs about 260 people.[50]

• Cerro Manganese Bronze Limited manufactures more than 200 alloys that conform to national, international, or customer specifications. The majority of its products include hollow rod, wire, and flats. Based in Ipswich, the firm's 189,000-square-foot plant has 185 employees.[51]

Both pages: Cerro Metal Products manufactures a wide variety of products, including brass forgings such as the one above. Headquartered in Bellefonte, Pennsylvania, the business was founded as Titan Metal Products in 1915.

## Anderson Copper and Brass Company

Spun off from the 1976 Cerro merger, Anderson went on to become a profitable firm in its own right after the reinvestment of its earnings for new and improved facilities and equipment.[52] It manufactures a wide line of brass connectors and valves used with soft metal and plastic tubing to transmit and control a variety of gases and fluids in both commercial and industrial markets.[53]

Headquartered in Oak Forest, Illinois, the firm operates a 77,000-square-foot[54] facility at its headquarters.[55] In addition, Anderson operates a plant in Hicksville, Ohio, and a distribution center in Frankfort, Illinois. Combined, Anderson's manufacturing and distribution centers occupy 175,000 square feet and employ approximately 250 people.

Opposite: Headquartered in Oak Forest, Illinois, Anderson Copper and Brass Company makes and sells a wide variety of fixtures, valves, and connectors.

# NOTES TO SOURCES

### Chapter One

1. Dick Griffin, "How Pritzker Buys a Firm," *Chicago Daily News*, 8 December 1977.
2. The Marmon Group 2000 Annual Brochure.
3. Ibid.
4. www.forbes.com, "The 500 Largest Private Companies in the U.S."
5. Bob Pritzker, interview by the author, tape recording, 18 January 2001, Write Stuff Enterprises.
6. Ibid.
7. Ibid.
8. Ibid.
9. Ibid.
10. The Colson Caster Corporation, "A Centennial History, 1885-1995," The Marmon Group archive.
11. Ibid.
12. Jack Steinberg, *The Making of The Marmon Group*, privately published by The Marmon Group, 1998.
13. Ibid.
14. Bob Pritzker interview, 18 January 2001.
15. Steinberg, *The Making of The Marmon Group.*
16. Steve and Lynn Culver, *Classic Bike*, July/August 1995.
17. Bob Pritzker, interview by Jack Steinberg, tape recording, 21 July 1992, Write Stuff Enterprises.
18. Bob Pritzker interview, 18 January 2001.
19. *A Review and History of the Colson Corporation, 1952 to 1957* (brochure), 24 July 1957, The Marmon Group archive
20. Steinberg, *The Making of The Marmon Group.*
21. Ibid.
22. Ibid.
23. Ibid.
24. Minutes of the Board of Directors of Great American Industries, Inc., 28 July 1955, The Marmon Group archive
25. Bob Pritzer, interview by Jon VanZile and the author, tape recording, 28 July 2001, Write Stuff Enterprises.
26. Ibid.
27. Ibid.
28. Bob Pritzker, interview by Jack Steinberg, tape recording, 23 July

1992, The Marmon Group archive.
29. Steinberg, *The Making of The Marmon Group*.
30. Minutes of the Board of Directors of Great American Industries, Inc., January 11, 1956, The Marmon Group archive.
31. Ibid.
32. Steinberg, *The Making of The Marmon Group*.
33. Ibid.
34. Bob Pritzker, letter to Great American Industries, Inc., shareholders, 30 June 1956, The Marmon Group archive.
35. Steinberg, *The Making of The Marmon Group*.
36. Bob Pritzer, interview, 28 July 2001.
37. Ibid.
38. Ibid.
39. Bob Pritzker, interview, 18 January 2001.
40. Steinberg, *The Making of The Marmon Group*.
41. Ibid.

**Chapter One Sidebar: Family**

1. Jon Anderson, "Pritzker on Pritzker: A mogul talks about his family dynasty," *Chicago Tribune*, 24 November 1985.
2. *Chicago Directory 1886* (Chicago: Lakeside Publishers, 1886), Chicago Historical Society.
3. *Who's Who in Chicago and Illinois* (Chicago: The A. N. Marquis Company, 1945), 721.
4. Ibid.
5. Ibid.
6. Bob Pritzker, interview, 18 January 2001.
7. Anderson, "Pritzker on Pritzker."
8. Bob Pritzker interview, 18 January 2001.
9. Marylin Bender, *At the Top* (Garden City: Doubleday, 1975), 305.
10. www.forbes.com, "500 Largest Private Companies."
11. Ford S. Worthy, "The Pritzkers: Unveiling a Private Family," *Fortune*, 25 April 1988.

**Chapter Two**

1. Steinberg, *The Making of The Marmon Group*.
2. Ibid.
3. George Jones, interview by the author, tape recording, 26 January 2001, Write Stuff Enterprises.
4. www.ladarling.com/history.htm
5. Steinberg, *The Making of The Marmon Group*.
6. Bob Pritzker, interview, 28 July 2001.
7. "Fact File: L. A. Darling Company," 1961, The Marmon Group archive.
8. Ibid.
9. Jay Pritzker, interview by Jack Steinberg, transcript, undated, The Marmon Group archive.
10. Ibid.
11. Bob Pritzker, letter to Colson Corporation employees, 16 May 1960, The Marmon Group archive.
12. "Darling Corp. Acquires Colson," *Elyria (Ohio) Chronicle-Telegram*, 21 September 1960.
13. Bob Pritzker, interview by Jack Steinberg, transcript, undated, The Marmon Group archive.
14. Jones, interview, 29 January 2001.
15. Steinberg, *The Making of The Marmon Group*.
16. Bob Pritzker, interview, 28 July 2001.

17. "Darling Buys Big Marmon Interest," *Chicago Sun-Times*, 3 January 1963.
18. Ibid.
19. www.iupui.edu/~harrold/indiana/marmon.html
20. Francis Chase, Jr., "Hell-on-Wheels Herrington," *Saturday Evening Post*, 8 August 1942.
21. Ibid.
22. Steinberg, *The Making of The Marmon Group*.
23. J. B. Long, letter to Col. A. W. Herrington, 2 November 1961, The Marmon Group archive.
24. Bob Pritzker, interview, 28 July 2001.
25. Steinberg, *The Making of The Marmon Group*.
26. Chase, "Hell-on-Wheels Herrington."
27. Steinberg, *The Making of The Marmon Group*.
28. Ibid.
29. Bob Pritzker, interview, 28 July 2001.
30. Ibid.
31. Jones, interview, 26 January 2001.
32. Bob Pritzker, interview, 21 July 1992.

**Chapter Three**

1. Steinberg, *The Making of The Marmon Group*.
2. "Fenestra Incorporated Products," unpublished, 12 August 1958, The Marmon Group archive.
3. Steinberg, *The Making of The Marmon Group*.
4. "Florida Firm Has 37% Share in Fenestra," *Chicago Tribune*, July 24, 1963.
5. Steinberg, *The Making of The Marmon Group*.
6. Ibid.
7. Jay Pritzker, interview.
8. Bob Pritzker, interview by Jack Steinberg, transcript, 23 January 1996.
9. Ibid.
10. The Marmon Group, Inc. (Michigan) Annual Report 1968, 10.
11. Ibid., 3.
12. Bob Pritzker, interview, 23 January 1996.
13. Steinberg, *The Making of The Marmon Group*.
14. The Marmon Group, Inc. (Michigan) Annual Report 1968, 1.
15. Steinberg, *The Making of The Marmon Group*.
16. The Marmon Group, Inc. (Michigan) Annual Report 1969, 1.
17. Bob Pritzker, interview, 28 July 2001.
18. Steinberg, *The Making of The Marmon Group*.
19. The Marmon Group 2000 Annual Brochure, 27.
20. Steinberg, *The Making of The Marmon Group*.
21. Ibid.
22. Ibid.
23. Ibid.
24. Ibid.

**Chapter Four**

1. Ibid.
2. lcweb2.loc.gov/cgi-bin/query/r?frd/cstdy:-@field(DOCID+pe0035)
3. Steinberg, *The Making of The Marmon Group*.
4. Bender, *At the Top*, 323.
5. Steinberg, *The Making of The Marmon Group*.
6. Bender, *At the Top*.
7. Steinberg, *The Making of The Marmon Group*.
8. Ibid.
9. Bender, *At the Top*.
10. Steinberg, *The Making of The Marmon Group*.
11. Bender, *At the Top*.
12. Steinberg, *The Making of The Marmon Group*.
13. Nancy Cardwell, "Cerro's Leadership Housing Is in Danger of Going Under, Filings with SEC Say," *Wall Street Journal*, 9 April 1975.

14. Jones, interview, 26 January 2001.
15. "Cerro Holders to Vote on Proposal to Merge with GL Corp. Unit," *Wall Street Journal*, 20 November 1975.
16. Ibid.
17. "Judge Refuses to Block Merger of Cerro Corp. with GL's Marmon," *Wall Street Journal*, 24 February 1976.
18. Gene Smith, "Cerro Stockholders Vote Company's End to Join Marmon," *New York Times*, 25 February 1976.
19. Ibid.
20. Steinberg, *The Making of The Marmon Group*.
21. Jones, interview, 26 January 2001.
22. Steinberg, *The Making of The Marmon Group*.
23. Bob Pritzker, interview, 28 July 2001.
24. Ibid.
25. Steinberg, *The Making of The Marmon Group*.
26. Ibid.
27. Ibid.
28. Ibid.
29. Marney Keenan, "A Man for All Challenges: Corporations, Embassies, Charities, Civic Institutions—Jerome Van Gorkom Has Managed Them All," *Chicago Tribune Sunday Magazine*, 2 October 1988.
30. Albert Z. Carr, *John D. Rockefeller's Secret Weapon* (New York: McGraw-Hill, 1962), 189.
31. Steinberg, *The Making of The Marmon Group*.
32. Keenan, "Man for All Challenges."
33. Ibid.
34. Bob Gluth, interview by the author, tape recording, 18 January 2001, Write Stuff Enterprises.
35. Steinberg, *The Making of The Marmon Group*.
36. Ibid.
37. Ibid.
38. Keenan, "Man for All Challenges."
39. Steinberg, *The Making of The Marmon Group*.
40. Ibid.
41. Ibid.
42. Keenan, "Man for All Challenges."
43. Steinberg, *The Making of The Marmon Group*.
44. Ibid.
45. Ibid.
46. Gluth, interview.
47. Gerald Shannon, interview by the author, tape recording, 26 January 2001, Write Stuff Enterprises.
48. Steinberg, *The Making of The Marmon Group*.
49. Keenan, "Man for All Challenges."
50. Steinberg, *The Making of The Marmon Group*.
51. Keenan, "Man for All Challenges."
52. Ibid.
53. Steinberg, *The Making of The Marmon Group*.
54. Ibid.
55. Ibid.
56. Ibid.
57. Ibid.
58. Carol D'Ascenzo, interview by the author, tape recording, 18 January 2001, Write Stuff Enterprises.

**Chapter Five**

1. John Dolan, interview by the author, tape recording, 17 January 2001, Write Stuff Enterprises.
2. Bob Pritzker, interview by the author, tape recording, 30 May 2001, Write Stuff Enterprises.
3. Gluth, interview.
4. Bob Pritzker, interview, 30 May 2001.

5. Raymond Avendt, interview by Jon VanZile, tape recording, 7 June 2001, Write Stuff Enterprises.
6. Dolan, interview.
7. Ibid.
8. Gluth, interview.
9. Bob Webb, interview by the author, tape recording, 18 January 2001, Write Stuff Enterprises.
10. David Dees, interview by the author, tape recording, 30 May 2001, Write Stuff Enterprises.
11. Bob Pritzker, interview, 30 May 2001.
12. Dees, interview.
13. Bob Pritzker, interview, 30 May 2001.
14. Webb interview.

**Chapter Six**

1. www.getz.com/co~hist.htm
2. Steinberg, *The Making of The Marmon Group*.
3. Ibid.
4. "The Getz Corporation," *InterChange: A Newsletter for Members and Friends of The Marmon Group*, November 1981, The Marmon Group archive.
5. www.getz.com/co~hist.htm
6. "Getz acquires Hungarian trading firm," *InterChange: A Newsletter for Members and Friends of The Marmon Group*, September 1989, The Marmon Group archive.
7. www.getz.com/co~hist.htm
8. www.marmon.com/Companies.html
9. www.marcapcorp.com/
10. "MarCap Corporation," *InterChange: A Newsletter for Members and Friends of The Marmon Group*, October 1997, The Marmon Group archive.
11. "Marmon Extends China Presence with Baby Food Producer," *InterChange: A Newsletter for Members and Friends of The Marmon Group*, June 1998, The Marmon Group archive.
12. www.marmon.com/Companies.html
13. Steinberg, *The Making of The Marmon Group*.
14. www.marmon.com/Companies.html
15. "Wells Lamont Goes to Space," *InterChange: A Newsletter for Members and Friends of The Marmon Group*, June 1994, The Marmon Group Archive.
16. "Wells Lamont," *InterChange: A Newsletter for Members and Friends of The Marmon Group*, January 1978, The Marmon Group archive.
17. Ibid.
18. Ibid.
19. www.marmon.com/Companies.html
20. www.tuc.com/
21. Ibid.
22. www.transunion.com/FactBook/
23. "Trans Union Buys Majority Interest in Hong Kong Credit Bureau," *InterChange: A Newsletter for Members and Friends of The Marmon Group*, April/May 1999, The Marmon Group archive.

**Chapter Seven**

1. "L. A. Darling Announces Purchase of Assets of Streater Store Fixtures," *InterChange: A Newsletter for*

Members and Friends of *The Marmon Group*, June 2000, The Marmon Group archive.
2. "L. A. Darling: A Century of Excellence," *Arkansas Tribune*, October 1977.
3. "L. A. Darling adds new companies, capabilities," *InterChange: A Newsletter for Members and Friends of The Marmon Group*, June 2000, The Marmon Group archive.
4. Ibid.
5. "L. A. Darling: A Century of Excellence."
6. "Darling Brings Other Businesses into Group," *InterChange: A Newsletter for Members and Friends of The Marmon Group*, June 2000, The Marmon Group archive.
7. "Restaurant Equipment Producer Joins Marmon," *InterChange: A Newsletter for Members and Friends of The Marmon Group*, November 1998, The Marmon Group archive.
8. "Prince Castle Buys Refrigeration Equipment Company," *InterChange: A Newsletter for Members and Friends of The Marmon Group*, January 2000, The Marmon Group archive.
9. "Notebook: Prince Castle, Inc.," *InterChange: A Newsletter for Members and Friends of The Marmon Group*, March 2000, The Marmon Group archive.
10. "Meyer Material Co. joins Marmon Group," *InterChange: A Newsletter for Members and Friends of The Marmon Group*, November 1983, The Marmon Group archive.
11. "Meyer Material Company," *InterChange: A Newsletter for Members and Friends of The Marmon Group*, July 1985, The Marmon Group archive.
12. "Notebook: Meyer Material Company," *InterChange: A Newsletter for Members and Friends of The Marmon Group*, January 2000, The Marmon Group archive.
13. atlasfasteners.com/
14. "Atlas Bolt & Screw buys two firms," *InterChange: A Newsletter for Members and Friends of The Marmon Group*, June 1991, The Marmon Group archive.
15. "Atlas Bolt & Screw Acquires Producer of Stainless Steel Fasteners," *InterChange: A Newsletter for Members and Friends of The Marmon Group*, August 1998, The Marmon Group archive.
16. atlasfasteners.com.
17. Steinberg, *The Making of The Marmon Group*.
18. www.deerwood.com
19. "Amarillo Gear Company," *InterChange: A Newsletter for Members and Friends of The Marmon Group*, April 1991, The Marmon Group archive.
20. "Amarillo Wind Machine Company," *InterChange: A Newsletter for Members and Friends of The Marmon Group*, June

1991, The Marmon Group archive.
21. "Amarillo Gear Company."
22. "Solidstate Controls, Inc.," *InterChange: A Newsletter for Members and Friends of The Marmon Group*, August 1998, The Marmon Group archive.
23. www.solidstatecontrolsinc.com
24. "Solidstate Controls, Inc."
25. www.uniformcomponents.com/
26. www.enersul.com/html/about/about_history.html
27. Ibid.
28. "1998 in Review," *InterChange: A Newsletter for Members and Friends of The Marmon Group*, February/March 1999, The Marmon Group archive.
29. www.enersul.com/html/about/about_history.html
30. www.marmon.com/Companies.html
31. "Koehler, Bright Star Merge, Begin Expansion," *InterChange: A Newsletter for Members and Friends of The Marmon Group*, August 1998, The Marmon Group archive.
32. "Koehler Flame Safety Lamps Carry Olympic Torch," *InterChange: A Newsletter for Members and Friends of The Marmon Group*, October 1996, The Marmon Group archive.
33. "Koehler, Bright Star Merge, Begin Expansion."
34. "Marmon/Keystone," *InterChange: A Newsletter for Members and Friends of The Marmon Group*, April/May 1992, The Marmon Group archive.
35. www.marmon.com/Companies.html
36. www.marmon-keystone.com
37. www.marmon.com/Companies.html
38. "Marmon/Keystone Buys Companies," *InterChange: A Newsletter for Members and Friends of The Marmon Group*, April 1995, The Marmon Group archive.
39. "Marmon/Keystone Adds U.K. Presence," *InterChange: A Newsletter for Members and Friends of The Marmon Group*, June 1997, The Marmon Group archive.
40. "Marmon/Keystone."
41. Steinberg, *The Making of The Marmon Group*.
42. www.marmon.com/Companies.html
43. www.futuremetals.com/pages/profile.htm
44. "Future Metals, a Distributor of Aircraft Grade Tubing, Becomes Member of The Marmon Group," *InterChange: A Newsletter for Members and Friends of The Marmon Group*, December 1996, The Marmon Group archive.
45. www.marmon.com/Companies.html
46. "Albion Industries joins the Group," *InterChange: A Newsletter for Members and Friends of The Marmon Group*, April 1990, The Marmon Group archive.
47. "Colson Acquires Conestogo Plastics," *InterChange: A Newsletter for*

*Members and Friends of The Marmon Group*, April/May 1999, The Marmon Group archive.
48. www.marmon.com/Companies.html
49. Ibid.
50. "Acquisition in U.K. Complements Colson Europe's Caster Business," *InterChange: A Newsletter for Members and Friends of The Marmon Group*, November 1999, The Marmon Group archive.
51. "Shepherd Products Brings Solid Reputation to The Marmon Group," *InterChange: A Newsletter for Members and Friends of The Marmon Group*, July 1990, The Marmon Group archive.
52. www.marmon.com/Companies.html
53. "Notebook: Industrias Metalicas Sudamericanas S.A.," *InterChange: A Newsletter for Members and Friends of The Marmon Group*, November 1999, The Marmon Group archive.
54. www.shepherd-productsinc.com
55. "Notebook: Shepherd Products, Inc.," *InterChange: A Newsletter for Members and Friends of The Marmon Group*, June 2000, The Marmon Group archive.
56. "Shepherd Hardware Products," *InterChange: A Newsletter for Members and Friends of The Marmon Group*, November 1998, The Marmon Group archive.

**Chapter Eight**

1. www.marmon.com/Companies.html
2. www.pearsalls.co.uk/backgr.htm
3. Ibid.
4. www.marmon.com/Companies.html
5. "Acumed, MicroAire, OsteoMed," *InterChange: A Newsletter for Members and Friends of The Marmon Group*, September 2000, The Marmon Group archive.
6. "Acumed Inc. Joins The Marmon Group," *InterChange: A Newsletter for Members and Friends of The Marmon Group*, July 1999, The Marmon Group archive.
7. "American Medical Instruments Joins The Marmon Group," *InterChange: A Newsletter for Members and Friends of The Marmon Group*, February 1995, The Marmon Group archive.
8. "Manan Medical Products Becomes Member of The Marmon Group," *InterChange: A Newsletter for Members and Friends of The Marmon Group*, August 1997, The Marmon Group archive.
9. www.mdtech.com
10. Ibid.
11. "What the Doctor Orders," *InterChange: A Newsletter for Members and Friends of The Marmon Group*, November 1999, The Marmon Group archive.
12. "Surgical Specialties Joins The Marmon Group," *InterChange: A

*Newsletter for Members and Friends of The Marmon Group*, June 1997, The Marmon Group archive.
13. "Notebook: Surgical Specialties Corporation," *InterChange: A Newsletter for Members and Friends of The Marmon Group*, January 2000, The Marmon Group archive.
14. www.marmon.com/Companies.html
15. www.bgsulzle.com/
16. Ibid.

### Chapter Nine

1. "Webb," *InterChange: A Newsletter for Members and Friends of The Marmon Group*, September 1981, The Marmon Group archive.
2. Steinberg, *The Making of The Marmon Group*.
3. Ibid.
4. "Webb Wheel Completes New Factory," *InterChange: A Newsletter for Members and Friends of The Marmon Group*, November 1998, The Marmon Group archive.
5. "Webb Wheel Will Add Production Capacity With Fourth Facility," *InterChange: A Newsletter for Members and Friends of The Marmon Group*, April/May 1999, The Marmon Group archive.
6. www.marmon.com/Companies.html
7. www.detroitsteel.com/
8. Steinberg, *The Making of The Marmon Group*.
9. "Detroit Steel Products," *InterChange: A Newsletter for Members and Friends of The Marmon Group*, March 1980, The Marmon Group archive.
10. Ibid.
11. Ibid.
12. www.detroitsteel.com/
13. www.marmon.com/Companies.html
14. Steinberg, *The Making of The Marmon Group*.
15. www.marmon.com/Companies.html
16. www.marmon-herrington.com/history.htm
17. Ibid.
18. Chase, "Hell-on-Wheels Herrington."
19. www.marmon-herrington.com/history.htm
20. Steinberg, *The Making of The Marmon Group*.
21. www.marmon-herrington.com/history.htm
22. Steinberg, *The Making of The Marmon Group*.
23. www.fifthwheel.com/
24. Steinberg, *The Making of The Marmon Group*.
25. "Fontaine Fifth Wheel," *InterChange: A Newsletter for Members and Friends of The Marmon Group*, July 1999, The Marmon Group archive.
26. www.fifthwheel.com/aboutfi.html
27. www.marmon.com/Companies.html
28. Steinberg, *The Making of The Marmon Group*.
29. Ibid.
30. www.fontainetrailer.com/Company_History
31. "Fontaine Trailer," *InterChange: A Newsletter for Members and Friends of The Marmon Group*, December 1997, The Marmon Group archive.
32. Ibid.

33. www.fontainetrailer.com/Company_History
34. www.marmon.com/Companies.html
35. "Perfection HY-Test Buys Majority Interest in China Factory," *InterChange: A Newsletter for Members and Friends of The Marmon Group*, February 1996, The Marmon Group archive.
36. Steinberg, *The Making of The Marmon Group*.
37. Ibid.
38. "Perfection HY-Test Buys Majority Interest."
39. www.marmon.com/Companies.html
40. Steinberg, *The Making of The Marmon Group*.
41. www.trianglegroup.com/history.htm
42. Ibid.
43. www.marmon.com/Companies.html
44. Steinberg, *The Making of The Marmon Group*.
45. www.amsafe.com
46. www.marmon.com/Companies.html
47. www.amsafecp.com/
48. www.marmon.com/Companies.html
49. www.arthurhart.com/ComHysto.htm
50. "Seat Belt Maker Am-Safe Makes Two Acquisitions," *InterChange: A Newsletter for Members and Friends of The Marmon Group*, October 1996, The Marmon Group archive.
51. www.marmon.com/Companies.html
52. "Notebook: Bridport Aviation Products," *InterChange: A Newsletter for Members and Friends of The Marmon Group*, March 2000, The Marmon Group archive.
53. Ibid.
54. www.marmon.com/Companies.html
55. www.utlx.com/who.html
56. "Union Tank Car," *InterChange: A Newsletter for Members and Friends of The Marmon Group*, June 1997, The Marmon Group archive.
57. www.marmon.com/Companies.html
58. "Union Tank Car."
59. www.procor.com/
60. www.marmon.com/Companies.html
61. www.utlx.com/history.asp
62. Ibid.
63. "Union Tank Car Acquires French Lessor of Tank Containers," *InterChange: A Newsletter for Members and Friends of The Marmon Group*, April/May 1999, The Marmon Group archive.
64. www.marmon.com/Companies.html
65. "Riding the Rails," *InterChange: A Newsletter for Members and Friends of The Marmon Group*, December 1996, The Marmon Group archive.
66. Steinberg, *The Making of The Marmon Group*.
67. www.marmon.com/Companies.html
68. www.safetydata.fra.dot.gov
69. "Riding the Rails."
70. www.marmon.com/Companies.html
71. "Marmon Transmotive buys Trackmobile," *InterChange: A Newsletter for Members and Friends of The Marmon Group*, July 1987, The Marmon Group archive.
72. www.marmon.com/Companies.html
73. Steinberg, *The Making of The Marmon Group*.

74. "Riding the Rails."
75. www.impulsenc.com/TMP953650685.htm
76. Ibid.
77. Ibid.

**Chapter Ten**

1. Steinberg, *The Making of The Marmon Group.*
2. www.cerrowire.com/
3. "Cerro Wire & Cable Co.," *InterChange: A Newsletter for Members and Friends of The Marmon Group*, March 1977, The Marmon Group archive.
4. www.cerrowire.com/
5. "The Marmon Group Adds Another Wire and Cable Company," *InterChange: A Newsletter for Members and Friends of The Marmon Group*, February 1998, The Marmon Group archive.
6. www.cableusainc.com/
7. Ibid.
8. "The Marmon Group Adds Wire and Cable Company," *InterChange: A Newsletter for Members and Friends of The Marmon Group*, June 1997, The Marmon Group archive.
9. www.gcicables.com/introfr.htm
10. www.marmon.com/Companies.html
11. www.getty.co.uk/about/
12. "Marmon Group's Wire & Cable Business Grows," *InterChange: A Newsletter for Members and Friends of The Marmon Group*, July 1999, The Marmon Group archive.
13. Ibid.
14. www.getty.co.uk/about/
15. "Marmon Group's Wire & Cable."
16. www.marmon.com/Companies.html
17. "Harbour Industries Joins The Marmon Group," *InterChange: A Newsletter for Members and Friends of The Marmon Group*, August/September 1994, The Marmon Group archive.
18. "Harbour Industries," *InterChange: A Newsletter for Members and Friends of The Marmon Group*, October 1996, The Marmon Group archive.
19. Ibid.
20. Ibid.
21. Steinberg, *The Making of The Marmon Group.*
22. www.rscc.com/pages/rscc.htm
23. Ibid.
24. "Marmon Group's Wire & Cable Business Grows."
25. Ibid.
26. www.rscc.com/pages/rscc.htm
27. Ibid.
28. "Hendrix Wire & Cable," *InterChange: A Newsletter for Members and Friends of The Marmon Group*, June 1998, The Marmon Group archive.
29. Ibid.
30. "Owl Wire and Cable, Inc. Joins The Marmon Group," *InterChange: A Newsletter for Members and Friends of The Marmon Group*, April/May 1999, The Marmon Group archive.
31. www.owlwire.com
32. "Owl Wire and Cable, Inc. Joins."
33. www.owlwire.com
34. "Owl Wire and Cable, Inc. Joins."
35. www.marmon.com/Companies.html
36. www.kerite.com/webpages/home.asp
37. www.marmon.com/Companies.html

38. www.invent.org/book/book-text/47.html
39. www.kerite.com/webpages/history.asp
40. www.pennaluminum.com/
41. Steinberg, *The Making of The Marmon Group.*
42. www.marmon.com/Companies.html
43. Ibid.
44. www.cerrocoppertube.com/
45. www.pmpa.org/mem/pmpanw.htm
46. www.marmon.com/Companies.html
47. "Acquisitions Add Business to Group," *InterChange: A Newsletter for Members and Friends of The Marmon Group,* September 2000, The Marmon Group archive.
48. "Four U.K. Businesses Join Marmon, Complement Cerro Metal Products," *InterChange: A Newsletter for Members and Friends of The Marmon Group,* February/March 1999, The Marmon Group archive.
49. Ibid.
50. Ibid.
51. Ibid.
52. Ibid.
53. Steinberg, *The Making of The Marmon Group.*
54. "Anderson Copper and Brass Builds Second Manufacturing Plant," *InterChange: A Newsletter for Members and Friends of The Marmon Group,* November 1998, The Marmon Group archive.
55. "Notebook: Anderson Copper and Brass Company," *InterChange: A Newsletter for Members and Friends of The Marmon Group,* July 1997, The Marmon Group archive.
56. "Anderson Copper and Brass Builds Second Manufacturing Plant."

# INDEX

*Page numbers for photographs are in italics*

## A

ABB Automation, 123
Absorbents Division, Graver Technologies, 105
Accurate Forging Corp., 137
acquisitions and mergers
   American Safety Equipment Corp., 57–58
   American Steel & Pump Corp., 49
   Cerro Corp., 51–56
   Colson Corp., 14–17
   Fenestra, 43–44
   GAI, 20–27
   L. A. Darling Co., 31–32
   Marmon-Herrington Co., 35–38, 41
   Mosaic Tile Co., 44
   Penn Brass & Copper, 56–57
   Service Caster & Truck Co., 18–19
   Trans Union, 58–64
   Triangle Auto Spring, 44–45
Active Gear Co., 116
Acumed, Inc., 100
Aetna Insulated Wire division, Cerro Wire & Cable, 126
agriculture equipment, 29–30, 40
Air Associates, Inc., 21–22
Alamo Water Refiners, Inc., 105–106
Albion Industries, Inc., 92, *92*
Altamil Corp., 114
Amarillo Gear Co. (*formerly* Amarillo Gear Works), 40–41, 88–89, *89*
Amarillo Wind Machine Co., 89
American Medical Instruments, Inc., 100–101
American Safety Equipment Corp., *57*, 57–58, 98, 117
American Steel & Pump Corp., *47*, *49*, 91
Am-Safe Bridport Companies, *108*, 117–119, *117–119*
Am-Safe Commercial Products, Inc., 117
Am-Safe Inc., 117
Am-Safe Textiles and Distribution, 117
Anbuma Group, 91
Anderson Copper and Brass Co., *138*, 139
Ansaldo Co., 123
Arthur Hart Webbing, 117
Associated Manufacturers International S.A., 41
Atkinson Finance Co., 29, 38
Atlas Bolt & Screw Co., *87*, 87–88
Austin Hopkinson Ltd., 43
Austins Marmon, 81

automotive and truck products, 56–58, *110–111, 115*
Avendt, Raymond, 70
Avery Flight Interiors and Safetywear, 117, 119
Azco Steel Co., 91

**B**

B. G. Sulzle, Inc., 103
Baxter Armstrong, 78
Beatrice, 72
Beijing Huilian Food Co., Ltd., 78
Bess Corp., 47, 49
bicycle division, Colson Corp., 17
bicycles and tricycles, 15, 17, *17*, 18
Black & Decker, 78
Boeing, 92
Bonser, Sidney, 62
Borden, 78
BP Amoco, 120
Braniff Airlines, 23
Bridport Air Carrier, 119
Bridport Aviation Products, 119
Bridport PLC, 117, 119
Bright Star Industries, 90
Britannic Aviation, 117
Bushwick Metals, Inc., 91
business strategy, 33–35, 69–73. *See also* management style
*BusinessWeek*, 64
Butler Manufacturing Co., 38

**C**

Cable USA, Inc., 129
California Institute of Technology, 14
Candy Fleet, 78
Cardair, 35
Cardair Division, Long-Airdox, 37
Cardox G.B., 35, 41, 43
Caruthersville, Missouri, factory, 33
Case Institute of Technology, 14
casters, *20–21, 92–95*
Castors International, 94
Celanese Chemicals, 120
Central Information System Co., 81
Cerro Copper Products Co., *50,* 51, 56, *134–136,* 134–137
Cerro Copper Tube, 137
Cerro Corp., *50,* 51–56, *52–55, 64*
  affiliated companies, 126, 130, 134, 137, 139
Cerro de Pasco, 137
Cerro E.M.S. Ltd., 137
Cerro Extruded Metals Ltd., 137
Cerro Manganese Bronze Ltd., 137
Cerro Metal Products Co., 51, 137, *137*
Cerro Precision Ltd., 137
Cerro Wire & Cable Co., 51, 126, *126–127*
Cerrocord division, Cerro Wire & Cable, 126
Cerro-Marmon Corp., 55
Cerrowire Division, Cerro Wire & Cable, 126
*Chicago Tribune,* 60, 64
Circle Wire Division, Cerro Wire & Cable, 126
Colson (Canada) Ltd., 20, 41
Colson Caster Corp., 92–94, *93–94. See also* Colson Corp.
Colson Caster Guangzhou, 92–94
Colson Corp., 13, *16,* 41, 44, 98. *See also* Colson Caster Corp.
  acquisition of, 14–17, 27
  bicycles and tricycles, *17,* 18
  casters, *20–21*
  divestitures, 17–18, 26–27, 32
  and GAI, 20–25
  labor relations, 25–27
  medical equipment, *19*
  relocation, 25–27, 32
  reorganization, 17–20
Colson Europe, 94
Colson Medical Instruments, 20
Colson Plastics Division, 92
Comtran Corp, 133
Conestogo Plastics, 92
Connecticut Telephone & Electric. *See* Contelco
Contelco, 21, 23–25, *24*
Co-op Screw Manufacturing Corp., 87–88

copper tube, *134–136*
Cottrell International, 103
cranes (construction equipment), *86*

## D

Darling, Lewis Archer, 31
D'Ascenzo, Carol, 65
Day, Austin Goodyear, 133
decentralization, 69–72
Dees, David, 71
Dekoron Division, Cable USA, Inc., 129
Densmore car, *58*
DePaul University, 22
Detroit Steel Products Co., 43, *44*, 110, 113
divestitures
    American Safety seat belt manufacturing, 117
    Bicycle division, Colson Corp., 17
    Illinois-California Express, 56
    James Mfg. Co., 38
    Jamesway, 73
    lift-equipment division, Colson Corp., 26
    Long-Airdox, 73
    Marmon Transmotive, 49
    Marmon-Herrington heavy-duty truck business, 37
    Oklahoma Steel, 49
    Pikrose & Co., 43
    Plastic division, L. A. Darling Co., 32
    Stylon Corp., 44
    truck division, Colson Corp., 26
    wheelchair division, Colson Corp., 17–18
Dolan, John, 69, 70–71
Dongguan Getty Electronics Products Co., 130
Dow Chemical, 120
dual reporting, 33, 35
Dunlap, John C., 45
Dunlap, Robert T., 21–25
Dynamic Logic, Ltd., 88

## E

Eastman Kodak, 78
Ecodyne Ltd., 106, *106*
EcoWater Systems, Inc., *96*, 104, 107, *107*
Elektromekan, 129
Elyria, Ohio, factory, *16, 20–21*, 25–27, 32
Emmert, L. William, 47
Enersul, Inc., 89–90
Enersul Operations, 90
Enersul Technologies, 90
Ericsson, 129
Erie Manufacturing Co., 14
Evans bicycles, 17
Evans-Colson bicycles, 17
Evans Products, 17
EXSIF SAS, 122
EXSIF Worldwide, Inc., 122, *122*

## F

Fairy brand tricycle, 15, *18*
Farm Equipment Acceptance Corp., 29
Fay, Winslow L., 15
Fay Manufacturing Co., 15
Fenestra, 43–44, *43–44*, 49, 56
financial data, Marmon Group
    1964, 41
    1965, 43
    1974, 49
    1976, 56
    1977, 57
    1981, 65
    2000, 73
First National Bank of Chicago, 16
Flagg Steel Products, 116
Fleetline Products, 114
foam rubber products, 26
Fontaine, John P. K., 114
Fontaine Fifth Wheel Co., 114
Fontaine International, Inc., 114
Fontaine International Europe Ltd., 114
Fontaine Modification Co., 114
Fontaine Specialized, 114
Fontaine Trailer Co., 114–116, *115*
Fontaine Truck Equipment Co., 114
Fontaine Fleetline Products, Inc., 114
food-service equipment, *85*

# INDEX

*Forbes* magazine, 13
*Fortune* 500, 51, 56
four-wheel drive, 35
Freightliner Corp., 114
Future Metals, Inc., 91, 92

## G

G. Mathes, 134
GAI, *13*, 20–25, 27, 32
Gallo, 78
General Cable Industries, Ltd., 129
General Electric, 61, 92
General Steelwares, 30
Getty Connections, Ltd., *128*, 129–130
Getz, Joseph, 76
Getz, Louis, 76
Getz Bros. & Co., Inc., *68*, 76–78, *76–78*
GL Corp., 52
Glass, Ed, 17
gloves, 79
Gluth, Bob, 59, *59*, 62, 65, 69
Golconda Corp., 55
Goodyear, Charles, 133
Graham, Stan, 14–15
Graham Metal Products Co., 30
Graver Technologies, Inc., 105, *105*
Graver Water Systems, Inc., 106
Great American Industries, Inc. *See* GAI
Green, Arthur, 19, 21
Guardian Fastener & Closure Systems, 87
Gulf American Land Corp., 43

## H

Hammond Corp., 78
Hanson, Chester A., 29
Harbour Industries, Inc., 130
Harding, Charles B., 55
Harig, Robert G., 46
Harroun, Ray, *36*
HDR Power Systems, Inc., 89
heavy-duty truck business, Marmon-Herrington, 37
Heineken, 78
Heinz, 78
Helene Curtis, 78
Hendrix, Bill, 131
Hendrix Wire & Cable, Inc., 130–131, *131*
Herrington, Arthur W., 35, 37, *39*, 113
Horwitz, William, 91
Huron Steel Co., 49, 91
Hyatt hotels, 23
Hy-Test Remanufacturers, 116

## I

Illinois-California Express, 56
Illinois Institute of Technology, 13, 64
Imperial Oil, 120
IMPulse NC, Inc., 123
Indal, 134

Indianapolis factory, 37–38, 41
Industrial Filter Division, Graver Technologies, 105
Industrias Metalicas Sudamericanas Limitada, 41, 94
Inter-City Auto Parts, 57
Intercooperation Co., 76
Invacare Corp., 17
Ion Exchange Division, Graver Technologies, 105
Iraqi Pipeline Co., 113

## J

James Foundry Corp., 29, 37–38, 40, 41
James Mfg. Co., 27, 29–30, 37–38
Jamesway, 73
Jamesway "Big J," 30, *30*
Jamesway Co. Ltd., 29, 30, 40, 41
J. B. Hunt Transport Services, Inc., 114
J. C. Penney, 31, 46, 79
JCB Electronica Industrial SRL, 89
Jones, George, 30, 32, 38, 46–47, 55–56, *59*, 65
Jonesboro, Arkansas, factory, 26–27, 30

## K

Kangol Magnet, 57
Kaszovitz, Josef, 56

Kenworth Truck Corp., 114
Keystone Pipe & Supply Co., 42, 47, *47*, 91
Knoxville, Tennessee, factory, 49
Koehler Manufacturing Co., 90
Koehler-Bright Star, Inc., 90
Kruizenga, Jack, 60

## L

L. A. Darling Co., *31–34*, 37, 41, *45–46*, *82*, 84
    acquisition, 31–32
    restructuring, 32–35, 45–47
labor relations, 17, 25–27
Lamont, Maurice, 79
lawsuits, 38
    Cerro Corp. acquisition, 56
    Fenestra acquisition, 44
    Marmon-Herrington merger, 38, 41
    Trans Union merger, 62, 64
    Triangle Auto Spring Co. antitrust suit, 45
Leader Metal Industry Co., Inc., 85
Lehman, Joel F., 56
Leonowens, Anna, 76
Lewin, Harold, 56
Lewin, Tannie, 134
Lewin, William, 134
Lewin Metals, 134
Lewin-Mathes Co., 134
Liddell-Birmingham Trailer Co., 114

lift-equipment division, Colson Corp., 26
Lindsay, Lynn G., 107
Liquid Filter Division, Graver Technologies, 105
L. J. Cohen Co., 134
logos
    GAI, *13*
    Getz Bros. & Co. Inc., *76*
    Jamesway, *29*
    L. A. Darling, *31*
    Marmon Group, *40*
    Marmon-Herrington Co., *35*, *113*
    Trans Union, *51*, *81*
    Webb Wheel, *49*
Londavia, Inc., 117
Long, John, 35, 49
Long-Airdox, 35–38, 41, 49, 73
Louis T. Leonowens (Thai) Ltd., 76

## M

Mack, Walter, 27
Mack Trucks, Inc., 114
Maidenform, 78
Malone, Dorothy, *17*
management style, 33–35, 40–41, 65, 69–73
Manan Medical Products, Inc., 101, *101*
manufacturing facilities
    Caruthersville, Missouri, 33
    Colson Corp., 15
    Elyria, Ohio, *16*, 19, *20–21*, 25

    Jonesboro, Arkansas, 26–27
    Knoxville, Tennessee, 49
    Paragould, Arkansas, 46
    Union Tank Car Co., *61*, *63*
MarCap Co., 78
Marmon, Walter C., 35, *39*, 113
Marmon-Bouquet France, 35, 41
Marmon College, 72
Marmon Group, Inc. (Michigan), 44–45, 47
Marmon Group, name, 40–41, 56
Marmon Motor Car Co., 35, *112–113*, 113
Marmon Sixteen, 113
Marmon Transmotive, 49, 123
Marmon Wasp, 35, *36*, 113, *113*
Marmon-Herrington Co., *28*, *35*, 35–38, *38–39*, 41, 49, *112–113*, 113
Marmon-Keystone Corp., 47, 91, *91*
Massey-Ferguson, 78
Matteson Metals, 37, 41
*McCall's* magazine, 23
McRobert Spring Co., 57
Medical Device Technologies, Inc., 101, 103
medical equipment, *19*, 78, *98–103*
mergers. *See* acquisitions and mergers
Mertz, Charles, 33

Meyer, Ben, 86
Meyer Coal & Material Co., 86
Meyer Material Co., 86, *86*
Michael Reese Hospital, 22
MicroAire Surgical Instruments, Inc., 98–100, *98–100*
Midwest Foundry Co., L. A. Darling Co., 31–32, *34*, 41
Mighty Lite Boat Docks, 116
Mighty Mouse rockets, 14, 22–23, 25, *25*, 26
Militair Aviation, 119
military vehicles, *38–39*
miner's cap lamps, *90*
mining operations, 51
M/K Express, 91
Mosaic Tile Co., 44
Murphy, C. Gordon, 52–54

## N

National Phoenix Industries, 27
Navistar International Transportation Corp., 114
*New York Times*, 56
NHD Group, 84
Ningbo Hongxie Machinery Manufacturing Co., Inc., 116
Nordyke and Marmon Machine Co., 113
Nortel, 129
Northern Ireland Exporter of the Year, 129
Northwestern University, 22

N.V. Jamesway, 30
Nylok Fastener Corp., *87*, 88

## O

Ohio Brass Co., 123
Oklahoma Steel Castings, 49
Olympic Games, 90, 123
OsteoMed Corp., 100
Owl Wire and Cable, Inc., *132*, 133
Owl Wire Logistics, 133
Oxford Tile Co., 44

## P

pacemakers, 78
Pacesetter, 78
paint roller business, 14–15
Pan American Screw, Inc., 88
Paragould, Arkansas, factory, 46
Pascale, Henry "Cap," 37–38, 41
Paveloc Industries, Inc., 86
PBN Medicals Denmark A/S, 101, 103
Pearsalls Implants, 98
Pearsalls Ltd., 98
Pearsalls Surgical, 98
Pearsalls Sutures, 98
Penn Aluminum International, Inc., 57, 134
Penn Brass & Copper, 56–57
Penn Machine Co., 122, *122*
Penske, 114

Pepsi Cola, 27
Perfection American, 116
Perfection HY-Test Co., 116, *116*
Perrier, 78
Peruvian nationalization, 51
Peterbilt Motors, 114
Pikrose & Co., 43
pipe and tubing, *91*
Plastic division, L. S. Darling Co., 31, *34*
PMC Corp., 130
Powers, Neely, 17
Prado Hermanos & Cia S.A., 41
Precision Edge Surgical Products, 98
Precision Weaving, 117
Premise Networking cables, 130
Price, Norman, 25, 38
Prickett, Bill, 64
Prince Castle, Inc., 85, *85*
Pritzker, A. N., 13, 17, 21, 22–23, *41*, *64*
Pritzker, Anna Cohn, 22
Pritzker, Bob, *12*, *14*, *59*, *64*, *70*
   Cerro Corp., 51–56
   Colson Corp., 14–20, 25
   education, 13–14
   family history, 22–23
   GAI, 20–27
   James Mfg. Co., 29–30, 38, 40
   L. S. Darling, 31–35
   management style, 40, 69–73
   paint roller business, 14

Trans Union merger,
58–64
Pritzker, Donald, 23, *41*
Pritzker, Harry, 13, 23
Pritzker, Jack, 13, 23, *41*, 64
Pritzker, Jay, *12, 14, 41, 59,
64*
    Colson Corp., 14–20, 25
    death, 23
    family history, 22–23
    GAI, 20–27
    intellect, 13
    Trans Union merger,
      58–64
Pritzker, Nicholas, 13, *22*,
22–23
Pritzker, Sophia
    Schwartzman, 22
Pritzker & Pritzker, 23
Pritzker method, 15–17
private company, Marmon
    Group as, 48–49, 62,
    71–72
Procor Ltd., 89, 120
Procor Sulfur Services,
    89–90
products
    agriculture products,
      29–30
    automotive and truck
      equipment, 56–58,
      *57, 110–111, 115*
    bicycles and tricycles, 15,
      17, *17*, 18
    brass products, *137–138*
    casters, 19, *20–21,
      92–95*
    copper tubing, *52–54,
      134–136*
    cranes, *86*
    Fenestra steel windows,
      43
    Flagg Steel Products, 116
    foam rubber products,
      26
    food-service equipment,
      85
    four-wheel drive, 35
    hand trucks, *20–21*
    Jamesway "Big J," 29–30
    Marmon Wasp, 35, *36*,
      113, *113*
    medical equipment,
      *98–103*
    Mighty Lite Boat Docks,
      116
    Mighty Mouse rocket, 14,
      22–23, *25*, 25–26
    miner's cap lamps, *90*
    pipe and tubing, *91*
    Premise Networking
      cables, 130
    radar control equipment,
      24
    railroad equipment,
      *120–123*
    retail store mer-
      chandising
      equipment, 31, *32*,
      45–46, *82–83*
    right-angle spiral-bevel
      gears, *89*
    screws and bolts, *87, 88*
    seat belts, *57, 118*
    Spacer Cable, 131
    sulfur processing, *90*
    Switchmaster railcar
      mover, 123
    tank cars, *58, 59, 61, 62*
    Triangle Air Springs, 116
    Viz-U-Sell, 31, *33*, 46
    water treatment
      products, *96,
      104–107*
    Webb wheels, *48*
    wheelchairs, 18–*19*
    wires and cables, *124,
      126–128, 131–133*

## Q

Quaker Oats, 78
Queen's Award for Export
    Achievement, 129

## R

radar control equipment, *24*
railroad equipment, *120–123*
Railserve, Inc., 123
Ravens, Inc., 116
Reagan, Ronald, *17*
retail-store merchandising
    equipment, 31, *32*,
    45–46, *82–83*
Rexnord, 116
right-angle spiral-bevel
    gears, *89*
Roadgear, 114
Robertson, Inc., *87, 88, 88*
Rockbestos Co., 52, 130
Rockbestos-Surprenant
    Cable Corp., 130
Rockefeller, John D., 58, 120
Rockwood & Co., 37
Rogowski, Walter R., 47, 65,
    71

Romans, Donald B., 60
Rosen, Leonard, 43
Royal Caribbean Cruise Line, 23
Rubatex, 21, 25, *26*, 27
Rumney, John G., 110
Ryder, 114

## S

Safetywear, 117
Salomon Brothers, 61
Sanford Day Co., 37–38, 41, 49
Schneider National, 114
Schulwolf, Sully, 56
screws and bolts, *87, 88*
seat belts, *118*
Service Caster & Truck Co., 18–19
Shannon, Gerald, 62
Shea, Cort, 17
Shell Oil, 120
Shepherd, George, 94
Shepherd Caster Corp., 92, *92*, 94, *95*
Shepherd Hardware Products Ltd., 95
Shepherd Products, Inc., 95, *95*
606 Matteson Street Co., 37
Solidstate Controls, Inc., 89
Solidstate Controls, Inc., de Argentina SRL, 89
Spacer Cable, 131
Specialty Bolt & Stud, 88
Specialty Steels, 91
Spectrum Labs, Inc., 105

Spezialfilterbau Walter Beck, 105
St. Jude, 78
ST Microelectronics, 129
Standard Oil, 58
Standard Oil Trust, 58, 120
Stanford Medical School, 64
Stanley, Trowbridge, 31
Steinberg, Jack, 15, 21, 37, 59, 76
Sterling Crane, 86, *86*
Stevens-Lee Co., 85
Store Opening Solutions, Inc., 85
Streater, Inc., 84
strikes, labor. *See* labor relations
sulfur processing, *90*
Sulzle, Benjamin, 103
Surgical Specialties Corp., *102–103*, 103
Surprenant Cable Corp., 130
Swift Transportation, 114
Switchmaster, 123

## T

tank cars, *58, 59, 61, 62*
Technical Textiles, 117
The Kerite Co., 133
*The Making of the Marmon Group*, 15–16
The Sloane Group, 85
Thorco Industries, Inc., 84
Tiger Industries, 90
Tiger-Sunbelt Industries, 90
Titan Metal Products, 137
Trackmobile, Inc., 123

Trans Union Corp., *51, 60, 70*
acquisition, 58–65
affiliated companies, 105, 106, 107, 120
Trans Union LLC (*formerly* Trans Union Credit Information), 62, *74*, 81, *81*
Transamerica Leasing, 73, 122
Triangle Air Springs, 116
Triangle Auto Spring Co., 44–45, 57, 116, *116*
Triangle Suspension Systems, Inc., 116, *116*. *See also* Triangle Auto Spring Co.
Triangle Suspension Systems, Ltd., 116
tricycles. *See* bicycles and tricycles

## U

Unarco Industries, 84
Uni-Form Components Co., 89
Union Tank Car Co., 58, *59*, 61–63, 62, 107, *120–121*, 120–122
Union Tank Line, 58, 120, 122
unions. *See* labor relations
United Cigar-Whelan Stores, 27
Unitherm Division, Cable USA, Inc., 129

University of Illinois, 14
University of Zurich, 14
Upjohn, 78

**V**

Van Gorkom, Jerome, 58–61, 64
VBG Ltd., 114
Vennard & Ellithorpe, 89
Viz-U-Sell, 31, *33*, 46
Volkswagen, 56–57
Volvo Trucks of North America, 114

**W**

*Wall Street Journal*, 55, 56
Wal-Mart, 47
water treatment products, 96, *104–107*
WCTU Railway, 123
Webb, Bob, 71, 72
Webb Wheel Products, Inc., *47–49*, 49, 110, *110–111*
Welch, Jack, 61
Wells, W. O., 79
Wells Lamont Corp., *69*, 78–79, *79*, 81
Wells Lamont Europe Industrial Division, 81
Wells Lamont USA, 81
West Coast Fasteners, 87
Westinghouse Air Brake Technologies, 123
wheelchair division, Colson Corp., 17–18, *19*
Wheeler Group, 91
wires and cables, *124, 126–128, 131–133*
Workwall division, L. A. Darling Co., 31
Worthington Manufacturing Co., *15*